United Arab Emirates Central Bank & 9/11

U.S. & U.K.
Authorities Shut Their Eyes!

Iqbal Ismail Hakim

GAAP Publishing House
A division of GAAP Corporation

United Arab Emirates Central Bank & 9/11

Book design Rebecca Hayes, Cedar Hill Publishing

Cover design by Rebecca Hayes, Cedar Hill Publishing

Published in the United States by
GAAP Publishing House
A division of GAAP Corporation

Visit www.uaecentralbankand911.com

Email the author at iqbalih@yahoo.com

ISBN: 0-615-12709-6

AUTHOR'S APPEAL TO UNITED NATIONS, HUMAN RIGHTS ORGANIZATION & THE WORLD AT LARGE

I am the auditor who had picked up the core 9/11 financing, which was remitted by some mysterious people in the UAE to Marwan Al Shhehai. As per US Authorities, Marwan was the pilot of United Airlines Flight 175 (the second plane) to hit World Trade Centre 2 South Tower at 9.03 on the fateful morning. The funds were remitted through the UAE Exchange Centre's Dubai Branch to Marwan in Florida. Subsequently the exchange's bank account in New York was frozen by the US District Court of NY and I understand court proceedings are held in camera and not made public. The then US Treasury Secretary, Paul O Neil along with his team visited the Exchange in Dubai for around twenty minutes and I do not know what was their conclusion.

All I know it that my life and that of my family changed drastically with threats of all kind. I have not seen my seventy plus mother and other family members living in India since then. The UAE Central bank did not take any action against terrorist bank accounts and other questionable funding picked up by me during the course of audit of various institutions operating in the UAE. My contract was terminated and when I protested threats from them started – "We will get you by hook or crook.". I understand a red arrest warrant has been posted in India to nab me.

I had approached the Governments of UAE, India, UK and the US authorities but in vain and as a last resort approached international press. I contacted practically all top news papers and channels without any success however Wall Street Journal came out with a story on September 17, 2003 and which is reproduced with their permission at the end of the book. I was also interviewed by Home land Security officers and FBI , who then approached Federal Reserve Bank officers armed with my reports but hold your breath nothing happened. Somebody somewhere was shielding the UAE and its questionable banking institutions.

While surfing the net I came across an interesting story but I do not know how far it is true – Following Osama Bin Ladin's outburst against the Americans, the Pentagon drew up plans to fire cruise missiles at a camp in Afghanistan's Helmand province which was frequently visited by Osama but at the last minute the strike was called off out of fear that it could kill an Emiri Prince / other UAE Officials. The story also goes further with the then CIA director testifying later " You might have wiped out half of the royal family in the UAE in the process" US officials believe this was a lost opportunity to kill Osama before the 9/11. Another reason for canceling the attack was that UAE had agreed to buy F16 aircrafts from the US and was America's best counterterrorism ally in the Persian Gulf. Well if you sell lot of arms to the Middle East, then one has to pay a price like seen in Iraq.

It is wrong to associate Islam with terrorism and there are countless examples in world history – the killers of Lincoln, Kennedy, Mahatma Gandhi or the Gandhi family Indira and Rajiv were not muslims nor was the Oklahoma bombing the handicraft of Islamic terrorists, although I agree there are black sheep but these are found everywhere some of them have been exposed in my book. Insulting religious books like Koran and the Bible will not end terrorism. One way of eliminating or reducing terrorism is to attack terrorist funding and through my book which is based on my reports, memos and observations I am exposing some of them along with some very powerful black sheep coming from various continents of the world including the US, UK and Middle East.

The Wall Street Journal had checked up my integrity, honesty and credentials from the UAE Central Bank and HSBC in London prior to going ahead with their article. I had picked up that HSBC was involved in massive money laundering operations, maintained accounts for questionable persons and terrorist entities besides violating US/ US sanctions for oil financing.

Following the Enron saga, honest auditors are required in the corporate world and if they are threatened and hit below the belt then why blame Arthur Andersen? All I need is justice and criminals booked. My family and I have paid a very heavy price for my honesty.

Somebody has rightly said that a country is born in the hearts of the poets, but is actually developed in the hands of politicians. I was under the impression that politicians from Asian countries have corruption flowing in their blood, but I was wrong. Corruption in the western countries is at the *highest* levels. Politicians, Auditors, Bankers and the media are equally responsible for terrorist attacks because of their attitude of looking the other way while it is the common people who suffer.

APPEAL TO THE INDIAN GOVERNMENT

I had approached the Indian Embassy in Abu Dhabi and in Washington with my plight, but unfortunately, there were no positive results. The Secretary of the Ambassador in Abu Dhabi told me that the case was a sensitive one and could adversely affect diplomatic relations with the UAE Government.

I had passed on all information to the Embassy in Washington, including reports of massive money laundering from an Indian Bank in Calcutta. The Embassy official indicated that no red arrest warrant was pending in India to nab me, but the Embassy would not officially confirm this in writing.

Indian Muslims often feel that they are subjected to step-motherly treatment. Although I do not believe this, it appears to have some weight as no response was received from various letters written to important political officials in India. My only question to the Indian Government is:

What is the need of maintaining good relations with a country which has sheltered well-known criminals wanted in India , ruins the Indian economy through the use of the Hawala System of remittance, millions of innocent Indian citizens are living a life of hell in UAE prisons (read stories about their plight in www.uaeprison.com), exploitation of Indian workers including thousands of Indian girls dancing in the UAE bars (the Indian Government has recently passed a law prohibiting girls from dancing in beer bars).

Non Resident Indians (NRI's) should not be treated as a cash cow for the billions of dollars remitted to India, but their problems should be looked into seriously.

I come from Mumbai and my birthplace was literally under attack from terrorists living in the UAE. The many pleas from the Indian Government to the UAE to hand over the criminals were completely disregarded and ignored. I am sure if Bal Thackeray was the Prime Minister of India, he would have attacked the UAE to capture the terrorists and I would have supported his decision.

Some years back, a tiny country like the Philippines fought with the UAE administration and secured the release of its citizen, who was employed as a maid in UAE and had killed her employer who had tried to rape her.

I have not committed any crime, but have exposed criminals including those who are related to 9/11. India should be proud of me because a country is not rich by the number of sky scrapers it has but by the character of the people who live there, and nations die when the character weakens. I am sure the Indian Government will roll out the red carpet to welcome me.

APPEAL TO THE UAE GOVERNMENT

I gave twenty years of my youthful life to the UAE and had I lived anywhere else, I would have been a senior citizen enjoying all state benefits, but your questionable

Governor of the Central Bank, (who actually should be behind bars for turning blind eyes to massive money laundering by the HSBC, the bank has agreed to maintain bank accounts for terrorists, arms dealers and other shoddy persons including violating US / UN sanctions) throws an honest auditor who picked up the 9/11 financing and other questionable transactions. His running of the Central Bank was sometime back criticized by the State Auditing Board.

In May 2005 he has committed another stupid deed by imposing fine on some UAE Banks which were violating share lending norms. By keeping the name of the erring banks as secret, there was a negative effect on the stock market with massive fall in the share prices of all UAE banks. Just imagine all UAE banks were punished instead of the handful. The dishonest Governor has to justify to all the banks operating in the UAE, as to why no action was taken against HSBC which agreed that it was involved in money laundering and other questionable activities.

Further the Governor has more faith in the Hawala System than the UAE banking system which he has been controlling for the last 12 years or so – A very sorry state of affairs indeed. If you need Hawala to run your economy then all the banks operating in the UAE should be shown the door and it will be nice to see worldwide oil exports financed through Hawalas.

The Hawala System has been ruining the economies of India, Pakistan etc and has been misused by drug dealers in the UAE and Hawala deals to Iraq during Saddam Hussein's regime were violating the US / UN sanctions. The Governor has been organizing International Hawala Conference every year to throw wool in the eyes of the world.

According to him Hawala is a very old system of remittance and is justified. Somebody should tell him that prostitution is also the oldest profession but is banned by most of the civilized countries just as Hawala is banned by most of the countries in the world. US Authorities have recently announced that they would go after Hawalawallas in the Middle East based on their finding that it has been extensively used by terrorist organization.

Please also ensure that threats to me and my family members are stopped.

DEDICATION

The book is dedicated to my family members who stood by me during my difficult times.

Special Thanks

- To Dana of Books Just Books for overall guidance
- Matt Pramschufer of Budget Media Design for designing the website
- Wayne Madsen, Indira Singh, Ronald Brewer for moral support
- Ateeq Mirzaand for proof-reading and suggestions
- Special thanks to Marty Sorenson and Becky Hayes at Cedar Hill Publishing for all technical help in bringing out this book.
- Mark Bewawi of Houston Radio for interviewing me on his talk show
- Rachel Ehrenfeld for her valued support and writing an excellent foreword.
- The Wall Street Journal for coming out with an article based on my report and for the permission to reproduce the same in my book. Also thanks to Paul Beckkit and Glen Simpson.

Table of Contents

FOREWORD

Iqbal Ismail Hakim has apparently done what no other insider to the United Arab Emirates (UAE) banking system has done before him. He seemingly exposed the sanctioned ongoing money laundering activities in the Emirates. Such an exposure in and by itself would have been important during peacetime, but it is critically important when we are working to keep money out of the terrorists' hands.

A lot has been written about Saudi charities and banks that forwarded money to the 9/11 terrorists. Yet, we heard very little about the role that the UAE banking and Hawallah systems had and continue to have in facilitating money laundering and terror financing. The UAE is not alone. International Western banks are taking advantage of the laissez faire attitude in the Emirates to conduct illegal money transfers with impunity. This book should generate enough attention to help eliminate such conduct.

Iqbal Hakim paid dearly for his courage. He lost his job and had to flee for his life, and even now he and his family remain under threat. Bringing this information to the public is critical to efforts to cut off terror financing.

Dr. Rachel Ehrenfeld
Author of ***Funding Evil; How Terrorism is Financed – and How to Stop It*** (Bonus Books 2005) and director of the American Center for Democracy.

INTRODUCTION

I have spent a significant portion of my life in the United Arab Emirates (UAE) and as such have seen and heard a lot about this lovely country. I can confidently say that if there is a paradise on the earth then it has to be UAE. I have some lovely memories of my association as an expatriate employed in the financial and banking sector, which among others included my last stint as the Chief Examination Officer with the UAE Central Bank's Banking Supervision & Examination Department.

Rags to riches stories are plentiful here. Some of today's big business barons of UAE started their careers either as salesmen, kitchen boys, butchers, or radio repairers and eventually found gold. Like millions of expatriates coming here to seek greener pastures, I too came here with a lot of dreams and wishes. This is perhaps summed up in the following poem I wrote:

ALL THAT I WANT

The World's wealth in my pocket
Kohinoor diamond in my locket

World beauties around me
The World's army under me
A million airplanes parked at my palace
A trillion dollars in my bank balance
Taj Mahal and Big Ben in my back yard
A hundred bodyguards from Scotland yard
Sun and moon dancing to my wishes
Queen of Hearts giving me kisses
Lions and Tigers in my lap
Hundred servants running at my clap
Breakfast in New York and lunch in Rome
Only after hundred years, I return home
Tons of gold in my locker
Pele as my tutor for soccer
A thousand Rolls Royces to ride
Million Princesses dying to be my bride.

Yes, UAE is a dream country to live in and a perfect place to enjoy life to the fullest. After all you have only one life to live.

The falcon is the national bird of the UAE and is literally worshipped and highly pampered in this part of the world. I am told that the price of a falcon ranges from $10,000 - $200,000 and sometimes even more. The falcon has extraordinary eyesight and is used for hunting down small animals.

An Auditors eyes are like the eyes of the falcon and are quick to spot any irregularities and deficiencies on one hand and appreciate strengths and merits on the other. This book is written not with a view to criticize the lifestyle in the Emirates, but an attempt is made to pinpoint certain issues in UAE's banking and financial world, which should be addressed so as to ensure that UAE remains among the top countries in the world.

UAE is comprised of seven emirates- Abu Dhabi, Dubai, Sharjah, Ajman, Um Al Quwain, Ras Al Khaima and Fujairah. Each Emirate has its own ruler but the ruler of Abu Dhabi is also the President of the UAE. Abu Dhabi is the capital of UAE and is the "Manhattan" of the Arabian Gulf. Sheikh Khalifa is the current ruler of Abu Dhabi and the President of UAE.

Sheikh Zayed Bin Sultan Al Nahyan, Sheikh Khalifa's father, who became the ruler some 35 years ago, overthrowing his brother, was a very smart politician and, following the growing American interest in the Gulf, post-Kuwait invasion, had loaned half a billion dollars (US) to the former Soviet Union. It was like protection money, but it was unfortunate that Russia broke into separate states and the loan remains unsettled on the books of a top Government owned Abu Dhabi based bank.

Another smart move was to politely refuse a US request to have a military base in Sadiyat Island on the pretext that the island was earmarked as a Free Trade Zone. Needless to say the free trade zone is yet to be born. However this smart man was completely deceived by a Pakistani banker who sold him some 77% of the shares of Bank of Credit & Commerce International (BCCI), which went down taking millions of depositors worldwide for a roller coaster ride.

BCCI had admitted, among other things, to laundering funds. Some 15 years later a prominent member of his clan finds himself in a similar soup, exposed to the world by the Wall Street Journal article of September 17, 2003, in its front pages. The article, which was based on the input provided by me, was a slap in the face to the UAE, which was hosting the 58th Annual meeting of the IMF and the World Bank.

Dubai (which is one of the seven emirates which comprises the UAE) is popularly called *City of Gold* and *Shopper's Paradise*, is a very modern city. Hold your heart. In an Islamic country you have a Hindu Temple near a Mosque, a wonderful example of freedom of religion and tolerance. It is a fact that the Sindhi (Hindu) community has played a major role in putting Dubai on the world map as an important trading city. Some of them are here for generations and were even richer than the then-ruler of Dubai.

The late Sheikh Rashid Al Maktoum and his sons have ruled Dubai pretty well. Sheikh Mohammad, the Crown Prince is a very dynamic person. A substantial credit for the development in Dubai during the last twenty years largely goes to him. I remember even today his masterstroke of starting Emirates Airlines by leasing four planes some twenty years back from Pakistan Airlines. His airline has not looked back since then while other airlines have been facing problems, more so after the 9/11 incident.

The Annual Shopping Festival started some nine years earlier is another feather in his cap when the entire city is decorated like a bride. The 58th Annual General Meeting of the World Bank and IMF (International Monetary Fund) was held in Dubai during September 2003, and sometimes I wonder that despite US authorities knowing fully well that a part of the 9/11 funding originated from Dubai, they did not boycott the venue.

Sharjah is another important emirate of UAE. I am very impressed with the University City, which is the brainchild of the Sharjah Ruler. Sharjah is an important venue for holding international cricket tournaments and can be called the Mecca of one day cricket. From time to time members of the international cricket community have raised match-fixing allegations with bookies holding the trigger to some nail biting matches, although nothing has been proved so far. Cricket lovers will always remember the famous India vs Pakistan match that was won on the last ball by Pakistani master batsman, Javed Miandad.

Fujairah is another tourist attraction with a lovely Corniche, ideal for honeymoon couples and an excellent resort. Although an Islamic country, UAE is becoming a paradise for attracting the criminal element. At every corner, one will find semi-naked prostitutes soliciting business, drugs are available everywhere. Very recently a group of grade-school youngsters, including girls, was arrested for drug related charges by the police, and last year a bunch of tourists belonging to top Indian families were arrested in a hotel with drugs.

To diversify income sources, some of the Emirates are aggressively marketing real estate projects to foreigners and investors. The country could soon be home to millions of people with questionable backgrounds.

Last year, rival Mafia shot down a prominent hotelier with Mafia links in broad daylight. Some years back a teacher, who also doubled as a human carrier for a Mafia group smuggling diamonds, was wiped out along with her entire family.

Other than Abu Dhabi, which is an oil rich emirate, the other emirates financial health is surviving to a large extent through Abu Dhabi paying their bills.

This generosity is solely attributed to Zayed's desire to stay together. I have doubts that his sons would be so accommodating since he is gone, and there is every danger that the union of these small emirates would be broken.

Dubai, which is the financial and trading hub of the United Arab Emirates has a beautiful creek, which separates the two prime areas Deira Dubai from Bur Dubai.

HSBC's main Headquarters is on the Bur Dubai side of the creek. Parked exactly before their headquarters is a beautiful traditional ship with the HSBC flag flying gracefully.

The ship is meant to entertain customers and other VIP's, and senior staff join in for some historical parties. I do not know the cost incurred to maintain this ship, but I know for sure no other bank in UAE has such a luxury. Yes HSBC has definitely taken a lot of people for a ride: the shareholders, customers, regulators and the governments of various countries.

Their Group Chairman and the Audit Committee in the UK were fully aware of the wrong doings at their UAE Branches, which included massive money laundering, violations of US and UN sanctions, defrauding insurance companies and bank customers and maintaining accounts for terrorists and arms dealers.

The HSBC Group management, instead of taking disciplinary action, and in some cases filing a police complaint against them, promoted key officials to very senior positions outside UAE, so that their lips would be sealed with honey forever. They made the auditor the scapegoat, and I was the auditor. The Russian Mafia attacked my audit partner Obaid Salami's house during the course of our examination. Obaid was so scared that he was forced by his wife to resign from the Central Bank at the first opportunity, while I continue to receive threats even to this very day.

There are many reasons for me writing this book, one of them is to redeem the image of auditor's, which has come under a lot of fire following the Enron saga and the numerous accounting scandals witnessed lately. I have been connected to the accounting and audit profession for nearly twenty-five years and, as such, I wish to pay back the profession I love.

HSBC UAE operations have been a hunting ground for laundering millions of dollars and when I picked up their dirty operations as a regulator from the UAE Central Bank, HSBC officials used all their muscle to harm my audit team members and me. Annual salary raises and promotions are a scarce commodity at the UAE Central Bank and so after one year I started job hunting outside UAE.

I was interviewed for a senior position at Saudi British Bank (an affiliate of HSBC) in Riyadh, which did not materialize. HSBC management claimed that since I was not offered the job (some two years before the investigations), I was taking revenge on HSBC UAE Branches. I leave it on the readers to judge whether I was taking revenge on them.

Another reason for this book is to tell employers to stop discrimination. Despite having the best qualifications in the UAE Banking Industry (Masters in Accounting & Finance, Certified Public Accountant, Associate of The Chartered Institute of Bankers and Company Secretaries) backed by two decades of experience I was given a very raw deal by the UAE Central Bank.

As per their policy manual, an employee having any one of the prescribed qualifications (ACIB, CPA, or CFA) is entitled to the "Special" grade and despite holding two of the approved qualifications; the special grade was not awarded. The Executive Director had recommended time and again to the Governor of the Central Bank to promote me in accordance with my qualifications, but without success.

Later on, when I was away on a long unpaid leave, the Governor took the opportunity to cancel my assignment illegally, as I knew too much about their dirty economy. My housekeeper, who managed my family members, was threatened and told to leave UAE within a week. In fact my seventy-plus mother kept on asking me what crime I had done that they were forced to leave UAE so quickly.

Well, my dear mother, the only crime your son committed was that he was an honest and fearless person. I had picked up that various banks in UAE were laundering millions of dollars, but the Iranian drug mafia used an Iranian Exchange in Dubai using Hawala (transferring funds through non-banking channels) transactions to move their dirty money. Further I had picked up that an Exchange in Dubai effected Hawala transactions to Iraq in violation of US/UN sanctions.

The core financing of the 9/11 attack was also spotted by me during the course of my audit of an exchange company in Dubai, which is primarily run by a Saddam Hussein look-alike.

HSBC officials and the Governor of UAE Central Bank, for their own selfish interests, have inflicted a wound on me and my family that may never heal. I had no option but to leave United Arab Emirates, which had been my home for many years. Don't play with the emotions of a bread winner, because if you hit him below the belt then only God can save you from his wrath. This book is a wounded person's response.

The Governor cancelled my contract and repossessed my new four-wheel car mortgaged to the bank, but completely forgot to take back the official laptop provided to me, which contained all the skeletons I had dug up during the course of my duties. My housekeeper mistakenly took the laptop away with her, which has enabled me to narrate my story with facts and figures so that powerful criminals are booked and justice served.

The UAE Central bank has challenged that they will nail me by hook or crook. Based on information conveyed to me, an Interpol Red Arrest Warrant is waiting in India to nab me. I would like to see which judge worth his salt will pass a judgment against an auditor who had picked up 9/11 terrorist financing, and who was always vocal against institutions helping drug dealers, terrorists and notorious arms dealers to wash their dirty money in UAE.

I am also appealing to the World Leaders to control their banking industries, because if you want to control terrorist activities, you must break their backbone by going after their funding. Don't shut your eyes or look the other way when an honest auditor like me picks them up. Events like 9/11 will continue to rock the world and the next target could be the Big Ben of London, Eiffel Tower of Paris, the Pyramids of Egypt or the Taj Mahal of India.

The book is also a wake up call to the worldwide regulators of the Financial Industry who it seems are sleeping even after my various SOS to them, or have sold their soul for a dime and are pimps on the payroll of some of the institutions involved in questionable deals.

I had also approached some of the top players in the media and the international press to break my plight to the world, but believe me the press is not an honest watchdog of the people, and instead of barking at the criminals are actually wagging their tail to show gratitude for the little bones thrown at them to keep their mouths shut. A reporter told me a bottle of wine is enough to intoxicate them and these institutions would gladly offer a whole vineyard.

The book is written in the public interest, to bring out the truth and to defend myself and restore my family honor, which has been badly tarnished.

To quote my favorite actor from the Indian film industry Mr Amitabh Bachchan, "If you keep quiet, the world will rub your face in the mud."

Hence, I have decided to speak up.

ANONYMOUS LETTER

It all started with an anonymous letter addressed to the Governor of the UAE Central Bank, in which the activities of Saeed Al Jabri were exposed. The letter stated that Jabri was defrauding banks in the UAE and his company, NEWS Shipping was in huge debt.

The UAE Central Bank is the Central Bank of the country but physically operates from a dingy place compared to the glittering skyscrapers found in Abu Dhabi. One of its main functions is to supervise all banks operating in the UAE. The Governor Sultan Al Suweidi runs this highly disorganized unit. He is currently serving his extended second term as the Governor and most of the employees at the Central Bank are looking eagerly forward to his exit.

Sultan was earlier the Managing Director of Abu Dhabi Commercial Bank for more than a decade and the employees celebrated when he moved to the Central Bank. [ADCB is one of the many local banks.] He is a self-centered autocratic leader with a passion for cutting staff allowances. Even while smiling, he is stingy and even his half smiles are reserved for only special occasions.

During his tenure at ADCB, very few employees were promoted or given the annual bonus. His first move upon joining the Central Bank was to cut down the existing housing allowances; furniture allowances and salary levels of the employees, including the lowest paid office boys. I personally know many employees who curse him even to this day. Even the terminal gratuity payable to an employee was drastically slashed.

He does not believe in delegation and most of his valuable time is spent on petty jobs, which include interviewing candidates for the lowest post of office boy, and approving petty bills. I distinctly remember that the sitting arrangement for the US Delegation led by then-Treasury Secretary Paul O'Neil was made by him nearly close to midnight.

The Governor recruited around 30 European Examiners some years back, owing to the international criticism following the near collapse of Dubai Islamic Bank and the sensational Madhav Patel episode in which 17 banks (including some prominent international banks) lost close to AED 1.0 billion. A lot of foreign banks were considering suing the Central Bank for poor supervision but dropped the idea since they wanted to continue their operations in this lucrative oil kingdom.

The Risk Bureau Department at the Central Bank produces on a quarterly basis a report detailing the top borrowers from the banking industry. This report was meant only for the Governor's eyes and not passed on to our Banking & Supervision Department. Allah only knows whether the Governor had any time left to read and review this report after spending valuable time on trivial matters. The exposure of the Banking community to Madhav Patel's Solo Industries was one of the largest, and morally, the Governor should have resigned.

In the middle of 2002, there was a huge cash fraud by some unhappy local UAE employees at the Dubai

Branch of the Central Bank, attributed to internal control weakness, and the Governor escaped again. Imagine cash fraud at the Central bank, which is the custodian of cash and foreign reserves of a country, besides being a banker to all the banks operating in the country. In any other country, the Governor should have been fired long ago, immediately after the near collapse of Dubai Islamic Bank. God only knows how he has survived all these scandals, and his presence continues to be a curse on the UAE Banking Community.

The Governor of UAE Central Bank is a strong supporter of the Hawala System, and in 2002, organized an International Hawala Conference in Abu Dhabi to strengthen his views that Hawala is harmless and should be legalized. My one and only question to my dear Governor is that if Hawala is legal then why should banks apply for a banking license in UAE, subject themselves to the rules and regulations of the UAE and foreign banks, and pay taxes on profits to the UAE Government when they can open a tea stall and also operate it as a Hawala House?

No, my dear Suweidi, you are just trying to protect your dirty economy, which to a larger extent runs on the smuggling business financed by Hawala. This underground money transfer business moves tons and tons of money without any trail anywhere, and is banned by practically all the civilized countries.

If Hawala is legal then, Suweidi, why don't you tell your oil companies to sell oil through Hawala? Why do they insist on financing through irrevocable confirmed letters of credit issued by acceptable international banks, and which have to be compulsorily confirmed by a local UAE bank? Why don't you issue a circular to all your oil companies and OPEC that in the future oil should only be sold through international Hawala and this has to be confirmed by a UAE counterpart Hawala dealer, duly registered with the Central Bank?

During my examination of various exchange houses, I had picked up that Iranian drug dealers wanted by the German authorities used Hawala to fund their trade, and Hawala transactions to Iraq were made in violation of the US/UN sanctions.

No action was taken against these exchange houses because as per the Governor, Hawala is a legal and legitimate way of doing business in the UAE. Most of the 30-plus European examiners are also cursing because hardly any one of them had an annual raise. It is a different story that most of them are useless and many of them were unemployed when recruited from Europe. In fact some of them don't even know the meaning of net-worth, or working capital and can't differentiate between a funded and un-funded exposure.

One of them was terminated for demanding a bribe from a prospective applicant for a Central Bank license. A couple of them report for duty under the influence of alcohol (a banned item in UAE). Some of them even date female employees of the bank they are auditing while some indulge in group sex by hiring prostitutes (which are available in every corner of UAE).

I personally know two local examiners were invited to one of the group sex sessions. The Governor always says that the European examiners are hired to train local UAE staff. I have to wonder what kind of training he is referring to.

On a couple of occasions when some of the local UAE staff had complained about the activities (drinking and sex) of these examiners, the Manager had dismissed these complaints with a casual remark, "This is their culture." These few people are actually spoiling the image of European community, but they hardly care as they know they were hand picked by the Governor, who would not like to admit that a grave mistake has been committed by hiring some of them.

The Governor on the other hand, sits in his ivory tower and has basically hired them to impress the Western World. A lot of banks have repeatedly complained that these expert examiners take six months for a normal audit, which causes them a lot of inconvenience.

The Governor it seems has an allergy to promoting people, and even the sacred UAE National employees are leaving the Central Bank one after another. In fact, a couple of them had voiced their grievances in the local Arabic newspapers some years back against Suweidi's policies. A very talented examiner approached the Governor for an increase in his pay packet. The next day, Sultan terminated that examiner and the poor chap realized that the world had fallen on him.

Just imagine your family is well settled and kids are going to school, and it is difficult to pack your bags and leave immediately. The examiner again approached the Governor and said, "I am withdrawing my request for the salary increase," to which the Governor replied then, "I am also withdrawing the termination letter." Such actions adversely impact staff performance.

Myself along with Obaid Salami were assigned by our Department to investigate this anonymous complaint. Our investigations led us to several banks in Dubai where Jabri and his company, NEWS Shipping, had small dealings. During the investigations it was revealed that Jabri was employed with HSBC Sharjah Branch, and hence our focus was shifted there.

Obaid Salami is a UAE National from Sharjah with eyes as sharp as a falcon and a brain that can outwit any fox. Unfortunately the Governor did not recognize Obaid's talents and his exit (like other promising nationals) further depleted Central Bank's resources. Unfortunately Sultan follows the policy of "penny-wise and pound-foolish" and somebody should make him understand that Central Bank should attract the best of talents since it regulates the banking industry. The numerous scandals and frauds in the UAE Banking industry (which are never disclosed to the world) can be effectively nipped in the bud if qualified staff is at hand.

It is a different story that Sultan does not want qualified personnel who would question his decisions. I was based in Abu Dhabi, which is the Head Office of the UAE Central Bank. Our investigations on Jabri's fraudulent activities at HSBC Sharjah, were made simple by an excellent internal audit report on the issue, and hats off to Phillips Dawe and his team. It is worth mentioning that as Regulatory Auditors, we rely a lot on the Internal Auditor's work for planning an engagement.

In this case, I also got a very important lead that Jabri was introducing Russian and CIS Customers to the bank (used to borrow funds from some of them) and Sharjah Branch might be involved in Bank of New York type controversy.

The HSBC Group later transferred key employees from UAE simultaneously and Phillips was one of them, since he knew and had pointed out that massive money laundering operations were being conducted from UAE Branches. Phillips was extremely helpful and agreed with our views on certain controversial accounts picked up by us. He knew too much of HSBC UAE Branch's dubious deals and was transferred to head their Indian Operations, a high-level position that will ensure that his lips would be sealed for the rest of his life.

We wrote a one-page memo to our Executive Director and attached a copy of the Internal Audit Report on Saeed Al Jabri's criminal activities. We never met Jabri, as he was reportedly serving a prison term for an unknown case, and HSBC later terminated Jabri's employment.

GOVERNOR'S
PACK OF CARDS

Sultan's pack of cards is comprised of three Aces - Saeed Hamiz, Abdul Rahim Sinkais, Saleh Allawi and the Queen of Hearts - Nariman Kamber. The rest of the pack consists of some 50 examiners, whom I refer to as soldiers thrown onto a battlefield to fight a losing war against money launderers, hawaldars (running the Hawalas) and hold your breath against the Governor Sultan, who always thinks his dollar is worth 110 cents while yours is only worth 90 cents. The department also has some six reviewers who oversee the examiners reports and give advice on banking matters from time to time. Most of them are aged and one of them is nearly deaf. It is a different story that most of their advice falls on the deaf ears of the Governor, who thinks himself to be a super-Greenspan.

Sultan lacks leadership qualities. I don't know whether he is alcoholic, but a bird did tell me about his special affinity with somebody at his previous position and if reports are to be believed, took her as his second wife. It seems taking a second wife is now a norm at the Central Bank – as they say follow the leader.

Sinkais, who follows the Governor faithfully like Mary's little lamb, is generally a nice guy but his mood changes drastically from time to time like the desert winds – at times he is pretty nasty, but at other times he is extremely friendly.

In one of his friendly moods, when we were invited by one of our colleagues, Khamis Bu Haroon (then a senior examiner) at his villa, for the traditional Ramadan Iftar dinner party, Sinkais took a dig at one of the officers, who was going for a second marriage. Sinkais narrated a very naughty joke, which I can never forget. The joke was about a UAE citizen who was about to take a second wife. He meets another UAE citizen who has abundant experience in managing two wives and inquires the secret formula. The second man declared that the formula to keep both the wives happy is "to sleep between the two of them at night." After six months the two men bumped into each other and our hero gets very angry and narrated how both his wives left him, when he was using his successful formula. To this the second man replied, "You misunderstood me. You see I have a house in Ras Al Khaimah, where my first wife lives and I work in Abu Dhabi where I have my employer-provided apartment, where my second wife lives, but at night I go to Dubai and stay in a hotel." Dubai is between Ras Al Khaimah and Abu Dhabi.

Khamis, who is ideal Governor material, had a clash with Sultan and like many other talented nationals, at the first available opportunity left the Central bank. He has both the qualities of head and heart and knows the pulse of the local financial sector. Nariman, a charming spinster matches her western outlook with modern dress code and generally shuns the Arabic Abhaya. She is a frequent visitor to the US having spent considerable time there for her higher studies.

She came to the Central Bank from Abu Dhabi Finance Department, some six years back and seemed quite enterprising but realized that Central Bank was not her cup of tea as Sultan clipped her wings quite early. The Queen Bee soon lost that enterprising spirit, the bold flair and the fresh outlook she brought to the department vanished into thin air and she was soon consigned to the back seat. Like Alice in Wonderland, Nariman was lost in the four walls of the third floor of the Central Bank.

We are lucky to have Saeed Hamiz as the Executive Director of our department. A person with a golden heart but unfortunately, he is very absent-minded and forgetful. He is as gentle as can be, but has a heart of gold and goes out of his way to help others.

Saeed has high regard for my capabilities and actually called me "Colombo". In fact, when he took over the department some six years back, somebody convinced him that I am the James Bond of the department.

Actually I have lived in the Emirates for a long time and my social circle was pretty big. UAE being a small country, news travels fast. On a couple of occasions, I had passed over some market information to the Department and one of my dear audit partners, SP Guha, started calling me "Bond 007".

This dear audit partner unfortunately was given a very raw deal and after nearly a decade with the Central Bank was so frustrated that at the first opportunity grabbed another offer. I have seen this partner (a Chartered and a Cost Accountant backed by an ACIB) with nearly thirty years of excellent banking record was forced to work under colleagues having absolutely no professional qualifications or record and my heart bleeds for him. His only fault was that, like me, he was an Indian.

In the UAE, changing jobs is very difficult for expatriate employees (A UAE Citizen can change jobs any time) since the first employer should have no objection and has a final say in the transfer of his employment visa. In many cases, the employer bans the employee from entering the UAE for six months; by affixing a no entry stamp in the employee's passport through the Immigration Authorities. All this discourages most employees from switching jobs.

So when Khamis left the Central Bank, to join other financial institutions, the loopholes in the laws were nicely used to avoid the six-month ban being imposed on SP Guha, so that he could join the new organization immediately. This was a double blow for the Central Bank, and also to me because I was close to both of them – SP was like a Dronacharya (a teacher) to me, as I had picked up a lot of the finer points of the craft from him.

Khamis had always been a lively audit partner with a generous heart. During my meeting with the Executive Director, I pointed out that Al Jabri had links with Russian / CIS Customers. A meeting was arranged with the Governor and the Internal Audit Report was shown to him, which mentioned the existence of some 300 accounts for Russian / CIS customers.

The Governor's attention was drawn to these accounts and I suggested that we review them because it was similar to the Bank of New York saga. This was agreed and Aboul Nasr Al Yousuf was now added to our audit team. He is a total team player, an extremely dedicated person with more than twenty years of association with the Central Bank. Unfortunately like most of us, he receives step-motherly treatment and was promoted only once. That too was by default, four years back, when the Governor decided to promote all those employees who were not promoted during the last ten years.

Once again I had to pack my bags for Sharjah and this time I had Nasr, who at that point was also based in Abu Dhabi. I would like to thank Nasr from the bottom of my heart, for being an excellent partner and putting in long hours during this assignment.

We really worked our hearts out and sometimes were the last people to leave the HSBC's premises at

Sharjah. I distinctly, remember the Credit Manager of the branch commenting that in his entire lifetime he has never seen auditors sitting so late.

Nasr is a very religious person and I don't think that he must have ever missed his daily prayers. Like me he talks straight from the heart and is very fond of smoking the Arabic pipe called Shisha over a cup of black coffee.

As we were spending time away from our home in Abu Dhabi, our family life was badly affected. The hard work took its toll and I was not surprised when Nasr told me that some serious differences had cropped up between him and his wife. I told him to call his wife over to Sharjah for a day and take her out for a good romantic movie in the evening.

His wife drove down along with their family cat, which resembled a mini-tiger. I am glad his family life was back to normal. This poem of mine is dedicated to Nasr, who comes from a beautiful country called Egypt and to all those at the Central Bank having two wives.

Double Trouble

My English friend tells his girl friend:
To kiss a Miss is a Comedy
But to miss a kiss is a tragedy.
My Egyptian friend tells his girl friend:
Darling come behind the Pyramid
And I will soon make you a Mummy
My American friend tells his girl friend:
My life is an envelope
On which I have written your name
With me, please don't play a double game
But all over, the girl friend always says:
Life is a game, if no pain then no gain
I recollect my Father would always say:
Life is a jungle when you are single

B'coz when you are double
You soon fall into a big trouble

I don't know what my father would have had to say about a person having two wives, but this is a prestigious possession in the Middle East and is as common as a person having two cars in the US. Later I came to know that Saeed also joined this elite ring.

L to R : Mabrouk, Iqbal Hakim, Saeed Hamiz
and Sultan Zaabi

Mabrouk, a senior examiner, complained to me during the HSBC examination that some of the western examiners were coming to work drunk. It is now a customary habit for some of them to take a break for a quick brunch and gulp a couple of pegs. The issue was discussed with Sinkais and Saleh Allaw, but none of them had the guts to take the matter forward. Even Sinkais had observed some of them coming drunk to the Central Bank time and again, but being afraid, did not complain to his master Suweidi.

Of the Western examiners, I will keep my money on Martin and Gary, who actually were being given a very raw deal by Suweidi. I was also impressed by the warmth of the sole Japanese reviewer, who approached me and said, "I like your reports. They are to the point, and the one involving the Prince is a collector's item."

HSBC SHARJAH

Farooq Arjoomand was then the Manager of HSBC Sharjah Branch and was pleasantly surprised to see us back at his branch after reviewing Jabri's case. As I was heading the audit team, I explained to him that in our second round, we would now be reviewing the 300 odd Russian / CIS customer accounts.

Farooq is nice and a pleasant UAE National, and we were assured the fullest co-operation. It was observed that most of these accounts were parked up at HSBC Sharjah and HSBC Deira Dubai Branches, so it was decided to review these branches. The Bank statements for the 300 customers were called for and these started arriving in batches.

Obaid started making friends at the Sharjah Branch and was told that Al Jabri was desperately trying to become a millionaire overnight and in this quest started a freight forwarding company called NEWS (North East West South) Shipping Company. This company soon got entangled in financial problems.

At the branch level, Jabri used his influence to get unauthorized overdrafts approved, and when the situation started getting worse, was forced to steal funds from customers' accounts. Apparently Jabri had the art of managing his colleagues with the result that the Branch Manager, Operations Manager and Credit Manager were all in his pocket, allowing Jabri to play his game. Even the collaterals advanced by him towards his exposure were returned / removed by him. Such was his hold on the branch.

The UAE Management later on served warning letters to these persons and terminated Jabri from service. Farooq was also transferred from the branch and we were invited to a farewell party hosted by the Sharjah Branch.

In his farewell speech Farooq mentioned that Central Bank was instrumental in his transfer. I would like to clarify that at that point our examination was at a very preliminary stage and we had no hand in his transfer.

In hindsight, by transferring him when the second round of audits had begun, I think the management acted wisely since the new man did not have any clue about the branch's prior misdeeds and was of very little help to us. Farooq was out of the picture and we now had to meet a lot of other officers to obtain their views on these suspicious accounts. I would like to point out that a lot of vital information is collected by auditors during these meetings, provided proper questions are asked and the officer in his quest to impress the auditor innocently passes on some other information.

One such officer who was heading the trade and finance department, was interviewed and to a question whether they opened any Letters of Credit (LCs) for any Russian / CIS Customers, replied in the negative. But added that the Department processed a lot of unusual documentary collections for Algeria. In view of his statement, we also added the "Algerian Connection" to our investigations.

We also met another officer who was heading the Al Imtiyas Accounts, meant only for high net-worth individuals. This person was highly critical of Al Jabri and about the millions of funds originating from Russia / CIS countries in dollars and remitted to HSBC Sharjah, using HSBC New York Branch. He was so scared that he mentioned that if the US authorities came to know about these transfers, HSBC would face closure in the USA.

He asked us to keep all the information gathered by us on these accounts strictly confidential. Well my dear friend, I am now forced to talk and the blame falls entirely on HSBC's management and on Central Bank's Governor.

HSBC Middle East Bank's controversial branch in Sharjah, Victor Bout entities banked here. Bout is reported to be one of the world's largest arms dealers and accused by UN of supplying arms and ammunition to rebels and terrorist organizations.

WE ARE LAUNDERERS BUT WON'T TELL THE UAE CENTRAL BANK

I had joined Central Bank with a lot of hopes, but soon realized that expatriate staff is seldom promoted and there is no annual raise in the salary packet. I have a habit of reading the Sunday Times of India, to keep close to home and in one of their editions came across an advertisement about senior vacancies at Saudi British Bank (a part of HSBC) in Riyadh. I knew the problems faced by employees desiring a switch-over of jobs in UAE and decided to try my luck in Saudi Arabia. My resume with an ACIB to my credit was helpful again. I was short-listed and directed to appear for an initial interview in Abu Dhabi. John Coverdale was then the Senior Branch Manager and he interviewed me.

The interview went on fine and I actually knew John since I was a member of the Central Bank Audit team, which had just completed the audit of his branch. Coverdale was impressed with my background and I was invited for a final interview in Riyadh. Based on my discussion with him, I came to know that a lot of British staff deputed to Saudi Arabia were keen to leave because of the prevailing strict culture and the Bank was looking for suitable replacements.

In Riyadh I realized that although technically I would be running the Advances Department, there would be two Saudi Nationals as the Manager and Deputy Manager. I demanded the same emoluments which they were paying to their British Staff deputed from the UK as I was not interested in selling myself cheap, noting the strict environment in Saudi Arabia.

After a week I was notified by their fax that I was not selected. Anyway, the two-day visit to Riyadh with all expenses paid by Saudi British Bank was a welcome holiday plus the bonus of visiting one of the holiest countries for a Muslim. My mother even to this day is happy that I bought two containers of the holy water called "Zamzam" for her.

After three years from the above job prospect in Saudi British Bank, I once again met John Coverdale, (along with my team) who now was the Chief Financial Officer of HSBC's UAE Branches. I actually had a soft spot for John and when we pointed out some controversial accounts picked up by us, he informed us that Jabri was the black sheep and they had referred the matter to their Chairman, John Bond, and he had probably reported the matter to Financial Service Authority, which was their lead regulator.

John assured us that this was one odd episode and otherwise everything was fine at their Sharjah branch. Further warning letters were issued to the key staff at the Sharjah Branch. He suggested that we meet David Bagley, who was the Compliance Head of the UAE and Gulf Region.

Later on, I realized that John had disclosed to his colleagues that since the HSBC Group did not hire my services, I was taking revenge on them. In fact, Abdul Jalil Darwish, the Executive Director & CEO of HSBC UAE Branches, came all the way from Dubai to Abu Dhabi to complain to the Governor about my taking revenge on HSBC.

I was asked by my department to defend myself and to this very day, I am defending myself. Loyalty to one's employer in the Middle East is taken very serious. By disclosing that I was looking for new opportunities, HSBC had destroyed my image. I have been overlooked for bonuses and even the grade which I deserved based on the Central Bank's guidelines were denied to me. At every opportunity the Governor called me the "Revenge Man".

In any other country, I would have instantly become famous, on picking up that one of the largest banks in the world was deeply involved in laundering funds.

We met David Bagley at his office and were told that remedial action was taken and there was no cause for concern. Upon review of his files, I picked up the following correspondence, which he had sent to his bosses in the UK confirming to them that they were launderers. I now leave it to the readers to decide if I am a Revenge Man or if problems did exists at HSBC UAE branches that were hidden from the Regulators and other interested parties.

Bagley also confirmed to me in his letter dated 30 March 2000 that they had not yet informed any of their regulators.

The various emails sent by Bagley to his bosses in London and other memos are given below and readers can form their own judgments.

General Letter
21Dec1999

Sent by: Sue M MILLINGTON

To: wright.s@mhub1.com
cc:
bcc:

Our Ref: MEM LGA 992597   Your Ref:
Subject: UAE - ML

Susan,

I have separately forwarded to Matthew a copy of GAM Investigation Report concerning certain events at our Sharjah branch.

This does touch upon activities on a number of accounts which were introduced by the employee who was the subject of the investigation.

I attach to the fax copy of this note a copy of the flow chart annexed to the report in question which shows transactions of a distinctly suspicious nature.

This particularly given the fact that the personal account shown into which the original transfers were made from MOD Azbekistan, and the Cyprus company, was opened by an individual who stated that he had an income of some USD1,000 p.m.

It is of course likely, if not inevitable, that the offending accounts will be closed.

As there is no money laundering law in the UAE no local regulation has been broken, and it may be that these particular accounts can be viewed as being part of misfeasance by a single employee. As such there is probably only slight risk of any external reputational damage.

I am told that our systems are not able to search for accounts which may have been introduced by this employee, and accordingly we will be left with having to go through an audit of other accounts opened for the nationality identified in the recent directive following the BONY case.

I do not propose making any report of an ML related nature to the local Central Bank, although a report will have to be made with regard to the staff fraud, and I will leave you and Matthew to determine whether you need to formally advise the FSA.

If you do perhaps you could let me know.

I will of course keep you informed as to the wider progress made with regard to the further enquiries into accounts maintained at SHJ.

Kind regards,

David Bagley.

Re: *Memo: Re: MONEY LAUNDERING ISSUES - UAE (David W J BAGLEY)*

 HSBC

Memo
30Dec1999

To: David W J BAGLEY@HSBC@HSBCMERIDIAN
cc: wright.s@mhub1.com
bcc:

From: Matthew J W KING AT HIBL-LONDON7@HIBCCMAIL   Tel:
Subject: Re: MONEY LAUNDERING ISSUES - UAE

David

Thank you for your update of 22 December 1999.

The fact that you have identified at least one group of accounts which
is almost certainly some form of laundering is of concern and, no
doubt, you are giving it the appropriate priority. I would be
grateful if you could keep Susan and I updated of developments. In
the meantime could you provide me with a brief summary suitable for
reporting to GEC and Group Audit Committee.

The issue of external interest is something which the FSA has focused
on very recently. I suggest you ask the HR department to confirm that
the GSM Section 6.5 is being complied with.

Regards.

M J W King

_____ Reply Separator _____
Subject: Memo: Re: MONEY LAUNDERING ISSUES - UAE
Author: David W J BAGLEY at HSBC
Date: 22/12/1999 05:27

Matthew,

I refer to your note to Susan.

I will attempt to answer your questions.

At present the MLCO is undertaking an urgent review of the 200-300
"Russian" accounts at SHJ branch. To put this in perspective many of these
accounts only hold small balances and probably relate to persons in some
form of employment locally. Some of that employment may be a little
informal, particularly for the women, but that in itself is not a huge
concern.

We have found at least two groups of accounts with fairly large balances

Memo: SHJ- Money Laundering (Annabelle RODRIQUES)

HSBC

Memo
02Jan2000

SHS M·L·f·le

To: George M SEQUEIRA/MGR OPS MEM/BBME/HSBC@HSBC
cc: John E COVERDALE/COO MEM/BBME/HSBC@HSBC
         dawe.p.a@mhub1.com
bcc:

From: David W J BAGLEY   Tel: 971 4 5077697
Subject: SHJ- Money Laundering

George,

Before the annual year end returns, and the Audit Committee meeting in February I would like to have resolved matters as far as possible.

Specifically I want to be able to report that in relation to Money Laundering we have:-

1. Complied with the relevant recommendations contained in GAM's report of December 1999, primarily paragraph 8, which I know you already have in hand.

2. I think we should take immediate steps to close the 4 accounts identified in the 'Semenchenko group" of accounts, and I would be grateful if you could advise me when this has been done. Given that the transactions uncovered by GAM already show suspicious activity I believe that we are already in a position to close the accounts. There is a risk of some fall out given the fact that there appear to have been dealings between Saeed Al-Jabri and the account holder. We will have to face this at some point and therefore I see no need for delay or further investigation of the account activity.

3.We should also search for any other accounts where any of the signatories are the same as any of those on the accounts already identified, and consider any such accounts for closure.

4. You may wish to consider interviewing SHJ staff to ascertain whether there were any other accounts with which Al-Jabri was closely involved as these may reveal irregularity. I would prefer looking at all accounts introduced or signed off by him but understand that this is not possible.

5. Whilst you are quite rightly concentrating on "Russian" accounts at present, we will need to consider to what extent there needs to be a review of all accounts at SHJ.

Clearly there are indications that there compliance with GPP's has not been what it should have been.

Whilst it is clearly not possible to look at every account again we should perhaps set a threshold in either balance or turnover terms for the review.

This will have to be done by SHJ and signed off by their management.

6. GAM's report also refers at page 12 to other accounts statements for which were found in Al-Jabri's desk,

Whilst there may be no concerns from an ML perspective we should still try and find out why statements were directed to the staff member.

I suspect that the above may not be an exhaustive list of actions, but I have tried to coalesce our various conversations into a clear set of steps.

I would welcome any comments.

Memo: Re: MONEY LAUNDERING ISSUES - UAE (David W J BAGLEY)

Memo

02Jan2000

To: Matthew J W KING AT HIBL-LONDON7@HIBCCMAIL @ HIBM@HSBCMERIDIAN
cc:

From: David W J BAGLEY   Tel: 971 4 5077697
Subject: Re: MONEY LAUNDERING ISSUES - UAE

Matthew,

I thank you for your GEM.

I am ensuring that the UAE MLCO takes sufficient early action to identify and close any further accounts where either we have not followed adequate KYC procedures and/or where there has been any suspicious account activity.

Whilst the initial focus will be on "Russian " accounts I intend following up with a review of a suitable sample of accounts across the board given the obvious potential for accounts of other nationalities.

The only account group where actual laundering has been identified was one closely associated with the member of staff who has already been dismissed. If this remains the case then other than a clear need to tighten opening procedures, increase awareness and the effectiveness of training and monitoring this incident may well be limited.

We will always be vulnerable to the activities of dishonest staff, particularly where their position enables them to exert control over branch activities.

For the purposes of GEC and Group Audit I would suggest the following, which assumes that a report from GAM will be submitted by Matthew:

" An investigation was carried out by GAM following the absconding of a member of staff , Saeed-Al Jabri who was bsed at SHJ branch.

The investigation report has been produced and as a result of the findings the member of staff has been dismissed.

During the course of the investigation statements relating to accounts managed by A Semenchenko were found in Jabri's desk.

Activity across the 4 accounts identified suggest some form of laundering, and the accounts have been closed.   *yet to be closed*.

A process of further reviews of accounts, account opening procedures, monitoring and training is underway, under the supervision of RMLCO given the general concerns which the Report raises concerning the level of compliance to GPP's at SHJ. "

Please let me know if you require anything further at this stage.

I will be participating in further meetings intended to address the wider control issues raised by the report.

Regards

General Letter: Money Laundering

CLOSED ACCOUNTS

HSBC ⟨X⟩

General Letter
24Jan2000

SHJ M/L

Sent by: Rita SKELSON

To: John E COVERDALE/COO MEM/BBME/HSBC@HSBC
cc: George M SEQUEIRA/MGR OPS MEM/BBME/HSBC@HSBC
  David W J BAGLEY/RLA LGA MEM/BBME/HSBC@HSBC
bcc:

From: Dilip HIREMATH Tel: 971 6 5090234
Our Ref: SHJ MGR 000068 Your Ref:
Subject: Money Laundering

This is further to George's Memo of 20JAN00 and the following is by way of first update:

-Letters for closure of account by 30 January 2000 have been dispatched to Mr. Semenchenko Andreii, San Air Gen Trdg. (WLL) FZE and Mr. Kakharov Mardiboy. JSM Gen Trdg had already been closed recently. (We have released block on San Air's current account against credit card outstanding of approximately AED30k in Semenchenko's a/c. However Semenchenko's credit card has been put on hot status to ensure no further billings.)

-Letters for closure of other eleven corporate accounts are also being finalized today and additional three accounts identified for closure are pending SHJ Mgr.'s return expected later this week for further endorsement.

-During the course of this week all non-borrowing accounts are being allocated to a relationship staff for review (and subsequent monitoring). We expect the review to highlight additional accounts to be closed and this exercise will be completed latest by 29 February 2000.

-We have reviewed corporate account opening procedures and these have been made more stringent to ensure that there is minimal risk of non-profitable/ suspicious accounts being opened hereon.

-Similarly, personal account opening procedures have been tightened. Yesterday, one Russian customer was denied approval to open an account due to lack of references.

-Letters for closure of five personal accounts are being sent out today. Additional twenty Russian accounts have been reviewed and will be closed. This will be over a period of time and in line with our discussion in the meeting on 20 January 2000. Numerous other accounts are under review and an update will be given shortly as to their status.

We would prefer to send these updates on every Sunday and accordingly, the next update will be sent on 30 January 2000.

Regards

Dilip Hiremath
Acting Manager

General Letter: ML TRAWL UPDATE (Fawzia ARIF)

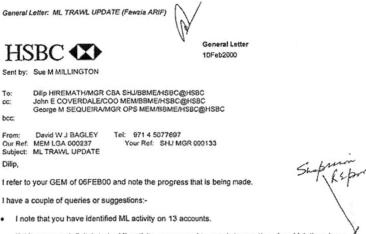

HSBC 〈X〉

General Letter
10Feb2000

Sent by: Sue M MILLINGTON

To: Dilip HIREMATH/MGR CBA SHJ/BBME/HSBC@HSBC
cc: John E COVERDALE/COO MEM/BBME/HSBC@HSBC
           George M SEQUEIRA/MGR OPS MEM/BBME/HSBC@HSBC
bcc:

From: David W J BAGLEY   Tel: 971 4 5077697
Our Ref: MEM LGA 000237   Your Ref: SHJ MGR 000133
Subject: ML TRAWL UPDATE

Dilip,

I refer to your GEM of 06FEB00 and note the progress that is being made.

I have a couple of queries or suggestions:-

- I note that you have identified ML activity on 13 accounts.

   If this appears definitely to be ML activity, as opposed to merely transactions for which there is no ready explanation, then I think you ought to give more details to George as they may require the lodging of a full exception under the ML reporting process. Could I perhaps leave you to discuss this with George as to whether such formal reports should be triggered.

- I note that you are in the process of contacting customers whose accounts you have decided to close.

   If it is likely that you are going to have a lot of accounts to close, I would suggest that you only interview those customers where an interview is necessary before you can reach a final decision as to whether an account should be closed or not.

   Where the decision has already been taken to close the account I would suggest that you merely send the standard letter giving them notice to close their account within 28 days.

   The only purpose of an interview is to determine whether or not an account should be closed, or perhaps in very exceptional circumstances where your relationship with the customer is such that you think you owe them the courtesy of a meeting.

   These meetings are fraught with difficulty, given that you have to be very careful to avoid saying any defamatory to a customer as justifying the basis for the closing of the account, which makes the mere despatch of a letter a much more manageable process.

Kind regards,

David Bagley.

General Letter
06Feb20C0

Sent by: Rita SKELSON

Tc   John E COVERDALE/COO MEM/BBME/HSBC
cc   George M SEQUEIRA/MGR OPS MEM/BBME/HSBC
        David W J BAGLEY/RLA LGA MEM/BBME/HSBC
bcc:

Our Ref: SHJ MGR 000133   Your Ref:
Subject: UPDATE DATED 06 FEBRUARY 2000

PERSONAL ACCOUNTS

- 26 Russian accounts have been closed.

- Thirteen potential ML accounts have been identified. Two of these account holders are presently being contacted directly.

- Account opening procedures remain stringent with four more requests by potential customers being denied due to inadequate documentation etc.

CORPORATE ACCOUNTS

- We are in the process of allocating all corporate accounts to relationship managers as requested by the Commercial Banking Champion. Upon completion of the review of accounts an analysis will be submitted to the Champion by 21 February.

- The above process will be combined with the ML exercise, which is already in progress.

Regards

Dilip Hiremath
Corporate Banking Manager

HSBC ◆

Mr Iqbal Ismail Hakim
Senior Examiner
Banking Supervision & Examination Dept
Central Bank of the U.A.E.
P.O. Box 854
Abu Dhabi
U.A.E.

30 March 2000

Our Ref : MEM LGA 000528

Dear Mr Iqbal Ismail,

Refer to our recent discussions concerning your investigations into matters at our Sharjah Branch.

I am writing to confirm to you that to date no formal written notification has been given either to the Financial Services Authority (the FSA), which is the HSBC Group's lead regulator, nor to the Financial Services Commission (the FSC) in Jersey, which is this Bank's lead regulator.

The FSC have been verbally advised, and there will be a meeting with them in early April to explain to them the detail of events at Sharjah.

A formal notification will shortly be forwarded to the FSA, and I will provide you with a copy once received by me from our Group Head Office.

Kind regards,

Yours sincerely,

D W J Bagley
Regional Legal Adviser

HSBC Bank Middle East
Middle East Management Office
PO Box 66, Dubai, United Arab Emirates
Tel: 971-4-535000 Fax: 971-4-531005
Telex: 45424 BBMED EM Telegrams: Bactria Dubai

*Incorporated in England by Royal Charter 1889
with limited liability*

HSBC DEIRA DUBAI BRANCH

Sayed Hashimi, a UAE National, was then-Branch Manager of HSBC Deira Dubai Branch. We were pretty surprised that for more than a decade he was holding this post. The basic internal control policy of rotation and transfer of staff was sadly overlooked, which contributed to the mess at his branch.

By the time we made our entry at his branch, word was out that we were investigating Russian accounts. We walked into his office one fine morning and introduced ourselves. Hashimi greeted us and his next sentence surprised all of us. I am quoting his historic famous words, " I know you are looking after Russian Accounts, but I will give you introduction to beautiful Russian girls."

Obaid, our local UAE partner in the team then gave him a lecture, which Hashimi will remember for the rest of his life. To quote Obaid, "Are you a Branch Manager or a pimp? Are you sure you are running a bank or a brothel?"

Nasr also got heated and angrily spoke something in Arabic and both stood up to leave the branch. Hashimi looked a worried man and said he was only joking. This statement only added fuel to the fire and Obaid got more furious and shouted, "How dare you joke with the Central Bank Auditors on the very first day."

I realized that the situation was getting out of control and requested both of them to sit down and told Hashimi to immediately apologize. Hashimi tried to cover up the situation and got up to offer the Arabic tea. Both Obaid and Nasr refused to drink the tea. To save further disgrace, Hashimi walked out of his office, which cooled the atmosphere in the room.

I took this opportunity to talk to my team members. I calmed them and reminded them of the need to examine the branch operations.

Hashimi's deputy came in the room and I requested him to make seating arrangements for my team and hand over the Russian / CIS related customer files.

After an hour or so, Hashimi came to us and did tender an apology for his morning's comment. I told my team to follow the policy of forgive and forget. Let me tell the readers that resistance / rude behavior are occupational hazards in an auditor's life. In our audit profession we make more enemies and fewer friends. I wish there were some laws so that we could sue people like Hashimi.

Later in the day, we saw Hashimi having a staff meeting, which was attended only by women. Nasr quickly spotted this and commented in Arabic to Obaid. In due course, we were told by one of their staff that ladies got frequently promoted in his branch.

We got friendly with one of their staff and came to know about their staff club and about the roaring time Managers and Officers had when they sailed for pleasure on HSBC's cruise ship, which remains permanently docked in the creek waters next to their Head Office in Bur Dubai. So now we knew what HSBC's ship was used for…

However this was beyond the scope of our audit, so we did not probe further, but it would be nice to know the cost and expenses involved to keep the ship floating, which in the end is passed on to the HSBC's shareholders.

The parties aboard the ship were further confirmed when one of their Sri Lankan lady staff members working at their Card center at Sharjah Branch was picked up by the local Sharjah Police for credit card fraud.

This lady was a very popular member of the staff club and in very good books of the senior officers attached to the Card center. She had their computer passwords at her fingertips, which she fully utilized to obtain duplicate credit cards for wealthy customers, and drew cash funds from different ATM's using the duplicate credit cards.

During the course of our investigations at their Deira Dubai Branch, I picked up the account of Leila Dadanavia, which had substantial funds coming in and going out at regular intervals. The officer handling this VIP customer was summoned and I inquired whether any KYC (Know Your Customer) profile was available on the customer. He replied in the negative but added that she is in business.

Obaid started laughing because Dubai is also famous for the hundreds of Russian girls working as prostitutes. The officer clarified that not in that business but she was in the perfume business.

At this point, Nasr inquired, "How do you know that?" The officer replied that the last time when she was in the branch she took out a perfume bottle from her handbag and sprayed on herself.

All of us had a hearty laugh at his answer and told him that every girl in UAE carries a make up set and perfume bottle in her handbag to counter the hot and humid climate. This was the level of KYC followed by the Deira branch. Later on David Bagley told us that the US authorities were looking for her.

Let me tell the readers that following the break up of the USSR, Dubai had become a hot place for people from Russia and other CIS Countries. Flights started arriving totally full with people bringing millions of dollars in cash to buy electronics, garments, clothes, perfumes and gold from Dubai for export to their countries.

There were no laws in the UAE to prevent people from bringing funds or declaring at the airports (in the US cash / travelers checks, etc., of over US$ 10,000 are to be declared). The officers at the UAE Airports would be overjoyed to see passengers bringing suitcases full of dollars in cabin handbags and welcomed them on the belief that they would shop from here and give the local trade a boost.

Believe me, there was a sudden boost in the export trade, and shopkeepers started learning the Russian language. The hotel industry in Deira Dubai got a tremendous boost as the wholesale market and gold market are located in Deira Dubai. Millions of dollars were partly converted into popular merchandise and exported to Russia/ CIS countries and partly deposited into banks. Converting hard dirty cash into liquid assets like gold or white goods is a device to launder.

HSBC Deira Branch was quick to spot the marketing opportunity and recruited a Customer Support Officer from one of the CIS countries to handle these customers. Some of these tourists started shell companies in the neighboring Sharjah emirates free zones. This explains the large number of Russian / CIS accounts at HSBC's Deira Dubai and Sharjah Branches. Once the bank accounts were established, incoming TT's were routed to their bank accounts in UAE from their overseas banks and in most cases using American based correspondent banks like HSBC New York.

HSBC also did business buying cash dollars from these customers and also opening new accounts to credit the proceeds. HSBC's Hexagon System, an Internet computer- banking product, was also marketed to them so that they could freely operate their account from their homes/shell offices to receive millions of dollars and remit the same outwards from their UAE bank accounts without even going to the bank. Some of the bank accounts became dormant with substantial balances in their savings / passbook/ fixed deposits and remained parked for tax reasons. There are no taxes in the UAE. They avoided paying taxes in their home country and enjoyed the loopholes in the UAE Banking System, since at that time there were no money laundering laws.

During a seminar on "Preventing Organized Crime" in Abu Dhabi in the middle of December 2002, top police officials of UAE had now admitted the existence of Russian/CIS mafia in the UAE, under the pretext of tourism and exports of electronic & electrical appliances. The officers had acknowledged that investments by these groups in real estate and other various commercial activities raised question marks.

HSBC Middle East Bank's Head Office in Bur Dubai – The mysterious salesman with annual turnover of $343 million (as reported by their Internal Audit Report) banked here. The management did not forward his file and bank statements to the Central Bank examiners despite repeated requests. The mystery remains who is this salesman? A terrorist, an arms dealer, a Hawaldar or a front man ?

A scene from Deira Dubai, the commercial hub, showing the traditional boats used for exporting merchandise to other Gulf countries like Iran, Iraq, Yemen, are mostly financed by Hawala. Reports indicate these are also used for drug trade and moving counterfeit merchandise. In the background are the Twin Towers of Dubai – HSBC has an office in one of these prestigious locations.

They will not meet the fate of NY's twin towers because UAE traditionally has sheltered some of the well known international gangsters, arms dealers, smugglers and with the opening of the real estate sector, notorious Alibaba's from every country together with their gangs of forty thieves will soon make hay, and no one destroys his own home and business empire.

This explains why there are no suicides or terrorist attacks in the UAE, which are now taking place everywhere.

RED FLAGS
OVERLOOKED

The term money laundering is believed to originate from Mafia ownership of laundromats in the USA. Laundromats, which can be found in every city and town in America, generate legal cash. This legitimate clean cash is mixed up with the dirty money obtained by the Mafia lords from gun-running, extortion and drug deals, prostitution and gambling operations, and deposited in the banks from time to time. Bank accounts are opened with various banks for the laundromat businesses and funds are deposited into these accounts, usually without any eyebrows raised. Interestingly many banks like HSBC Middle East have a policy of rewarding the bank staff for the amount of deposits they bring in but no carrot is offered to those who turn away business. This makes life pretty easy for launderers.

Another school of thought credits money laundering to China, where merchants hid their wealth for fear that the rulers would take assets they had generated and accumulated through business empires. They would convert money into readily movable assets or move cash to a foreign destination, mostly through Hawala.

In modern times, despite international bodies like the Financial Action Task Force monitoring the flow of dirty money around the globe, there are foreign destinations or countries that attract dirty money. Typically these foreign destinations are:

A) Countries with favorable tax systems or tax free countries like UAE. During the course of my duties as an examiner I have seen billions and billions parked in UAE banks as non-resident deposits for tax evasion motives.

B) Where financial institutions that receive dirty money pay only lip-service to anti-money-laundering laws or regulators like Suweidi turn a blind eye to my various memos.

C) Where sophisticated professionals such as lawyers, accountants and bankers are willing to help in hiding and laundering money or simply shut their eyes. Such professionals are a dime a dozen in the UAE.

Operating manuals of every bank includes scenarios where the bank may be used as a conduit for money laundering and staff are advised to exercise caution while dealing with such customers. The presence of any of these red flags do not necessarily mean that a customer is questionable, but it may however provide a reason to scrutinize the account more carefully. Some of the common red flags are given below:

- Customer has inflow of funds well beyond his stated income/resources.
- Customer has numerous deposits & withdrawals without apparent legitimate business purpose.
- Customer makes deposit by wire transfer and the funds are withdrawn immediately by cash/ wire transfer.

- Customer is reluctant to reveal any information concerning business activities or has difficulty in explaining the nature of his business when questioned due to lack of knowledge of the industry / trade.
- Customer has multiple accounts under one or multiple names and funds are moved from one account to another frequently.
- Customer has questionable background or is subject to negative news reports including possible criminal record / activities.
- Customer gives power of attorney to a third party and/or directs mailing of bank statements to a post box or gives instructions to hold the mail.

In light of the above, I am giving below some bank accounts picked up during the course of my investigations.

HSBC ⟨X⟩

Sent by: Dilani A FERNANDO

Memo
03Jun2000

To: George M SEQUEIRA/MGR OPS MEM/BBME/HSBC@HSBC
cc: John E COVERDALE/COO MEM/BBME/HSBC@HSBC
bcc:

From: Armaity NOOR Tel: 971 4 2074228
Subject: MONEY LAUNDERING - REVIEW OF RUSSIAN ACCOUNTS

George,

We refer to your memo dated 17th April, 2000 and subsequent discussions with C.K. Shah and the undersigned.

As requested in your memo, action taken on each of the MLSRs are summarised below alongwith our recommendations. It would be pertinent to mention however that the Bank was actively soliciting Russian business about 4/5 years ago with a Representative from Armenia cross-posted at the Branch for 2 years +. A lot of Russian business was put on our books at that stage.

1) A/C NO. 025-002023-130 IGOR MIKHITAROV

Account no.	Type	Currency	Outstanding	Status	Date a/c opened
025-002023-130	SSV	USD	12,967.65	Dormant	06.07.96
025-002023-281	TMD	USD	618,643.53	Active	04.05.98

- The account is mainly used for receiving IRMs which are later converted to TMD.
- The introducer's account (025-108614-001) has since been closed.
- The account turnover is not commensurate with the declared monthly income (AED20k-25k).
- Profession / Occupation as per Account Opening Application reads as General Manager and Owner of M/s TSE CEL, P.O. Box 600, 350062, Krasnodar, Russia.
- All our attempts to contact the customer on the available information have been unsuccessful.
- Special instructions to 'refer all transactions' have been loaded on all accounts.
- **We therefore recommend the MLSR status be continued till contact is re-established with customer.**

2) A/C NO. 025-044777 LIOUDMILA MINTCHENOK (AIG)

Account no.	Type	Currency	Outstanding	Status	Date a/c opened
025-044777-020	PSV	AED	392,764.92	Dormant	17.10.93
025-044777-251	TMD	AED	6,752,936.59	Unclaimed	12.12.95
025-044777-252	TMD	AED	2,786,554.96	Unclaimed	22.09.96
025-044777-253	TMD	AED	1,902,701.14	Unclaimed	12.01.97

- AIG Customer
- Large TMD's are placed with us by debiting PSV account.
- Husband & Power of Attorney holder is MD of a private airline in Russia (Elf Air).
- All our efforts to contact the customer on the available information have been unsuccessful.
- Special instructions to 'refer all transactions' have been loaded on all accounts.
- **We therefore recommend to continue the MLSR status till contact is established with customer.**

3) A/C NO.: 025-046053 EDOUARD A OGANESSOV

Account no.	Type	Currency	Outstanding	Status	Date a/c opened
025-046053-130	SSV	USD	216,413.82	Active	04.02.96
025-046053-281	TMD	USD	8,618.12	Unclaimed	11.03.97

Page: 1

HSBC's Deira Branch- Operations Examination.   **From 1-1-1999 to 13-06-2000**

058-454950-601	Gold Card	USD	0.0	Card revoked	Closed 31-03-99
058-454950-601	Gold Card	USD	0.0	Card lost	16-12-99
058-454950-601	Gold Card	USD	0.0	Card revoked	Closed 31-03-99

Problems with this account are:
- The customer is a Visa Gold Card holder.
- Credit card has been issued against a Time deposit for USD7500.0- held under lien.
- Account activity in Savings and USD account reflects mainly card settlements and activities.
- Profession/occupation as per Account Opening reads as businessman C/o Pirogova St. 6-60, 354000, Schop, Russia.
- HSBC have special instructions to "refer all transactions" , loaded on all accounts.
- In Nov '96 the client deposited cash USD50000.0, on Dec '96 another cash USD51000.0 was deposited. In February '97 he deposited USD32000.0 in cash. There were no activity after this until April 2000, when USD30000.0 was deposited and on the same day remitted the same amount to TL Motor Trading in Japan.
- HSBC were able to contact a friend of the customer from the Credit Card application who has informed them that the account holder is expected to visit Dubai around 15 June 2000. HSBC have diarised for further follow-up and will communicate when contact is established.

A/c No. 025-046780-020 Olga or Nikolai Dargonova (AIG)

Account no. opened	Type	Currency	Outstanding	Status	Date a/c
025-046780-020	Savings	AED	2433705.2	Active	08-11-93

Problems with this account are:
- HSBC, as a result of loading special instructions on the account, were able to interview the customer on her visit to the branch.
- Olga Trading which was earlier managed by the account holders (Olga D and/or D Nikolai) has since been closed and she is in the process of re-establishing the business.
- Special instructions to 'refer all transactions' have been loaded on all accounts.
- A cash deposit transaction of AED 200000.0 was questioned by HSBC when the client visited Deira branch, and the bank was advised that the money related to business activity performed by the customer from her personal account. Upon HSBC's refusal to accept business related transactions in her personal account as per Central Bank instructions, the client directly contacted the Central Bank on 14 may 2000. Mr Habib Kazim, at the Central Bank Dubai branch, (tel. 3939888)appeared to have been satisfied with the customer, and was of the opinion that business related transactions should be allowed in the customers personal account until she manages to re-establish the business. However, neither Mr Habib Kazim, or the customer, had reverted to HSBC, by the 31-04-2000. During HSBC's interview with the customer, she revealed that the funds lying in her account, are profits earned from earlier businesses and they were deposited with HSBC Deira branch for tax reasons and because of the insecurity prevailing in her country.

A/c No. 025-059023 Liobov Karivar

Account no. opened	Type	Currency	Outstanding	Status	Date a/c
025-059023-020	Savings	AED	1122059.6	Active	05-03-94
025-059023-251	Time Deposit	AED	386356.2	Unclaimed	25=04-95

HSBC's Deira Branch- Operations Examination.   **From 1-1-1999 to 13-06-2000**
058-457003-601   Gold Card   AED   0.0   Active

Problems with this account are:
- The customer holds a Visa Gold Card against a Time deposit of AED 300000.0 held under lien.
- Settlements of the credit card is done through auto payment from the (PSV) Savings account.
- The monthly income figure is not recorded on the account opening form.
- Although there are no manual instructions in the Savings account since the 23 January 1999, the account is not dormant due to system raised entries for card settlement.
- This non resident account holder is a housewife with no employment/income and an address in Russia. As of the examination date she has a credit card with a limit of AED300000.0, which is 100% secured by a cash deposit. Moreover, she has a Passbook Savings Account with a balance of AED 1100000.0, as of the examination date, which she uses to fund the credit card.
- All HSBC's efforts to contact the customer on the available information have been unsuccessful.
- As with other suspected money laundering accounts (MLSR status), special instructions to 'refer all transactions' have been loaded and HSBC have recommended MLSR status to be continued until contact is established.

A/c No: 025-063561 Mikhail Zaitchehko

Account no. opened	Type	Currency	Outstanding	Status	Date a/c
025-063561-050	Savings	AED	42730.22	Active	17-05-98
025-063561-251	Time	AED	140000.00	Active	21-05-20
025-063561-252	Time	AED	2579536.00	Active	01-12-98
058-457664-601	Gold Card	AED	0.0 Cancelled in Dec '98		
058-489527-602	Gold Card	AED	0.0 Cancelled in 23-05-00		
058-457664-603	Premier	AED	0.0 New Premier Card		

Problems with this account are:
- The was part of the initial list of accounts to be converted to Premier. The customer who deals on general merchandise including electronics and household furniture, visited the branch on 28 May 2000, and was interviewed by HSBC's Premier Officer. The client provided HSBC with copies of invoices in support of his business activities.
- The local contact address provided by the customer is Al Bros Trading Co. (Account No. 025-368663) who has a borrowing relationship with the branch.
- HSBC's premier/executives are fully satisfied with the explanations/ evidence provided by the customer, and have therefore recommended that this account be deleted from the money laundering list.

A/c No. 025-209032-252 Pavel Milosserdov.

Account no. opened	Type	Currency	Outstanding	Status	Date a/c
025-209032-252	Time Deposit	AED	402988.5	Active	05-05-98
025-209032-282	Time Deposit	USD	516817.4	Active	07-10-99
058-489527-601	CGI a/c	USD		Cancelled in April '99.	
058-489527-602	CGI	USD	0.0	Lost	
025-489529-603	CVG	AED	705.91(-)	Delinquent	

HSBC's Deira Branch- Operations Examination.   **From 1-1-1999 to 13-06-2000**
025-489427-604 HPR   AED   0.0   Uncollected
                                                   (new Premier Card)

Problems with this account are:
- Profession/occupation as per Account Opening Application reads as General Manager-Greenway Tourism and Cargo.
- This customer claims that his monthly income is USD20000.0, and the businesses annual turnover is USD 5000000.0.
- There have only been three transactions in the above accounts since June 1998, all of which have been deposits.
- The account was opened in April 1998 by depositing AED 366000.0 and in May 1998 a transfer of AED920000 was received from Citibank Dubai. In June 1998, he received USD235,000.0 from overseas, via an inward remittance. These monies were immediately converted into USD and have been kept in the above two Time Deposit accounts since this time.

HSBC were able to contact the customer on mobile telephone no. 050 6568323. He was not prepared to discuss any information over the telephone for security reasons. He informed HSBC that he would be visiting the UAE around the 15 June 2000. Must check to see the outcome of any interview?

A/c No. 025-278821-130 Nina or Vladimir Meshcherov

Account no. opened	Type	Currency	Outstanding	Status	Date a/c
025-278821-130	Savings	USD	9826.83	Active	03-05-99
025-278821-281	Time Deposit	USD	0.00	Closed	06-05-99

Problems with this account are:
- The savings USD account opened on 4 May 1999, show very transactions.
- The Time Deposit account has since been closed on 5 May 2000, and funds transferred to the Savings USD account as per customers written instructions.
- HSBC have also processed an Outward Remittance [ORM] for USD375000.0 from the Savings USD account as per customer written instructions (verbal approval from Mr Chandrasekhar with notes taken by Mr shirish Tamahane- CBA Manager).
- In view of the small current outststanding, HSBC recommended this item to be deleted from the Money Laundering list.
- These clients are residing in Cyprus and both work at Samara Currency Interbank Exchange. Vladimir works in the financial department, and Nina works for the Clearing House according to the account opening form.
- There was fixed term deposit at HSBC's Deira branc in Nov '99, for a sum of USD339000.0, which was transferred to Asia Europe Americas Bank in Seattle (Washington). The beneficiary was Arrowchiff Investments Ltd.

A/c No. 025-394289 Svatoslav Fyodorov

Account no. opened	Type	Currency	Outstanding	Status	Date a/c
025-394289-001	Current	AED	9827.46	Unclaimed	11-04-92
025-394289-211	Current Dep	USD	4116.49	Unclaimed	11-04-92
025-394289-282	Time Dep	USD	203469.76	Active	15-03-95

Problems with this account are:

GROUP AUDIT MIDDLE EAST **GAM GEN 000010**

GENERAL AUDIT OF HBME SHARJAH **MAY 2000**

3.5 Money Laundering Deterrence

3.5.1 Suspicious Transactions

Background

A considerable amount of work had recently been put in by MEM/SHJ to identify accounts on which suspicious transactions had taken place. As a result of the review around 50 accounts had been closed. This process was still continuing with two more accounts recently closed by the branch. Action had also been taken to improve overall controls. For example, all corporate non-borrowing accounts had recently been allocated to specific Corporate Relationship Executives/Officers who were responsible for monitoring the accounts more closely.

Finding

Notwithstanding the aforementioned, during the course of the audit the auditors were unable to obtain satisfactory explanations for the large turnovers/deposits passing over the following accounts:

Files & statements have been called for

A/c Number	FEB-APR00 Turnover (AED)	FEB-APR00 Balance (AED)	Name/ Designation	Monthly Income (AED)	Remarks
Personal A/cs					
040-025900-050	976,686	14,859	Al Wahesh Abdul Manager	Not stated on AOF	A/c opened 19FEB00
040-268427-001	36,783,850	45,274	Hamidevi Hamzah M. Director Flamingo Furniture Factory	10,000	-
040-191504-130	1,046452	5,857	Satourina Anna	Not stated on AOF	Transfers from Citibank
040-210767-050	1,232,202	9,064	Gupta Arun M. Director Gulf Trading	10,000	-

Note: Some AED 36.7 million ($10 million - USD) was routed through a personal account during the period of February to April 2000 and countless other accounts were noted by the Internal Auditors.

GROUP AUDIT MIDDLE EAST   —   GAM GEN 000010

GENERAL AUDIT OF HBME SHARJAH   MAY 2000

A/c Number	FEB-APR00 Turnover (AED)	FEB-APR00 Balance (AED)	Name/ Designation	Monthly Income (AED)	Remarks
040-232746-050	1,482,895	5,595	Faria Frederick M. Director Impact Furniture	Not stated on AOF	-
040-322612-050	2,621,130	44,666	Almulla Mohd Policeman	4,200	-
Corporate A/Cs					
040-105033-001	3,769,969	8,007	Al Nasser Diesel		-

(handwritten left margin: Files & statements have been called for)

Furthermore, the auditors could not obtain satisfactory explanations for the substantial cash deposits into passing over the following accounts:

Corporate Account	Cash Deposit MAR-APR00	Name/ Designation	Remarks
040-114340-001	AED709,000	Rocky Line Trading Est	Non-borrowing corporate
040-216806-001	AED525,000	Sky Air Cargo	Non-borrowing corporate

Risk

Reputational risk.

Recommendation

In liaison with MEM UAE MLCO, action should be taken to conduct a full review of the accounts detailed in the finding above.

In future, a HUB query report should be generated periodically (at least monthly) in accordance with the revised parameters recently agreed by MEM. Based on activity shown in this report action should be taken to investigate those accounts with unusual features/activity and to take appropriate measures to protect the Bank in accordance with the Bank's GPPs on Money Laundering.

THE MYSTERIOUS SALESMAN WITH $343 MILLION

HSBC Middle East Bank, at that time was just examined by the UAE Central Bank's examiners, which was a full scope audit and the KPMG boys had also finished their first half interim audit. I still fail to understand how both had missed some issues presented in their Internal Audit Report on the UAE branches.

One such report mentioned this mysterious salesman having an annual turnover in his personal account, which would earn the envy of many Middle Eastern Sheikhs. Despite repeated requests, HSBC Management did not provide us any details on his account and Wall Street Journal copied my memo in the front page of their Europe Edition on September 17, 2003, which was passed over by me to them. The world is eager to know who this salesman was and what was he selling? Perhaps drugs? Arms?

Or a Hawaladar involved in the Hawala business? Or a front man for some politicians or perhaps having links with the notorious Atomic Khan who had a connecting base in Dubai.?

The right person to reveal the mystery about this puzzle is Sir John Bond, who at that point was also the Chairman of HSBC Middle East Bank. Let us see whether Bond has any integrity and honesty left in his armory on which he gives lectures in HSBC's annual report.

Anyway, till he gathers courage to tell the truth to the world, read the excerpt from their Internal Auditor report on this super salesman. Every blue chip company would be out to recruit him at all costs, if that sum claimed by HSBC as his emoluments, including commission, is true. Imagine what must be the sales made by him for his employers!

The average monthly salary for a salesman ranges between Dirhams two thousand to Dirhams three thousand in Dubai (less than one thousand dollars per month, US).

The way HSBC is expanding its operations through new acquisitions, calling itself the world's local bank and winning countless awards like the best bank in the world, they definitely need such a "Salesman" in their team to market the banks products and services aggressively! So why not recruit him?

APPENDIX R

Suspicious Transactions

1.   020-102331-130 - Muhammad Rafiq

The account holder's occupation was stated as "Salesman". However, the turnover in the account was out of all proportion to the stated occupation.

For example:

     USD20 million in DEC97
     USD10 million in JAN98
     USD10 million in FEB98

(handwritten: Details have been called for)

HUB reports indicated annual turnover through the account at around USD343 million.

2.   Eurostar Communications - 020-158770
    Eurostar International   - 020-119459
    Saleh Al Hamady   - 020-173316
    Aston Technologies   - 020-261418

(handwritten: Star TV group)

All these accounts appeared to be linked. Substantial activity passed over each account, including the non-resident Savings Account of Saleh Al Hamady. Since facilities had been extended by DUB around six months ago to the first two companies, it is recommended that the legitimacy of funds flowing through each of the respective accounts is investigated, so as to ensure that cash flow is not being channelled out of the country for illegitimate/unknown purposes.

Excerpt from the Internal Audit Report on HSBC Dubai Branch.

OPERATION SPIDER WEB

Following the break up of the former USSR and the subsequent collapse of their economy, Russians and citizens of the newly created CIS countries were involved aggressively to move their money out of their country by hook or crook to avoid paying taxes and to wash the dirty money generated through prostitution, bribes, drugs, gun-running, extortion etc. Corrupt politicians and bankers who received a percentage for their services helped them in their mission.

As the US dollar was historically a strong and stable currency, funds were denominated in dollars and for clearing purposes were routed through the US banking system. The US banks, which acted as the correspondent banks, were keen to develop new business and looked the other way.

Later the funds would move out to tax shelters and countries with lax systems. In this way, millions and millions of dollars moved into the US and to avoid US taxation, funds would move to the next destination. UAE was one of them – a tax free country and with no questions asked by the banking community and regulators.

Some of the funds also moved back to Russia, making the incoming funds appear to be legitimate proceeds of business transactions. The Internet banking popularized by the banks to cut staff and other processing costs further helped the launderers. At the click of the computer mouse, one could electronically send millions of dollars to one country and minutes later, it could all be transferred into another account at a different bank or transferred out to a bank in another country. HSBC's HEXAGON system was nicely used by launderers to move funds, both incoming & outgoing.

This arrangement was prospering day by day and would have continued even to this very day except that one such transfer, as the story goes, was extortion related and the FBI was alerted. The probe revealed funds moving out to 45 countries like a web. The European countries also sprung into action after being alerted by the FBI, and in due course the operation got the nickname "Operation Spider Web." The operation was the biggest in the history of money laundering, leading to the arrest of a number of people.

The operation reached its zenith when a former NY banker and her spouse pleaded guilty to money laundering charges and admitted being involved and receiving a cut for the money transferred.

Some reports suggest the bulk of the money involved may have been part of loans advanced by international authorities for the reconstruction of Russia and looted by corrupt officials. However, the authorities in Russia denied these allegations. The mystery remains unsolved as powerful persons and top banks that were caught in the spider web pulled stings at right places and eventually the investigating web operations broke into pieces.

It is strange that the US regulators did not impose any fines on banks in the US having links with Russian bank accounts, including the latest ABN AMRO scandal (exposed in September 2004) but entered into a side agreement with the offending banks like it did with HSBC Bank USA in New York. The agreement revolves around the bank tightening its anti-money-laundering procedures and proper reporting of suspicious accounts to the authorities.

HSBC Middle East Bank admitted having 200-300 Russian / CIS related accounts, some of which were being looked into by the US authorities for funds transferred from HSBC USA Bank. The management did not forward us a list of those accounts on the pretext that HSBC USA was a separate entity, bound by confidentiality laws, and as such would not pass over any information to HSBC Middle East.

However, Bagley and Darwish did mention the account of Leila Dadanavai. HSBC's Internal Auditors for the Gulf region did make a passing comment in their report on Saeed Al Jabri's activities about the existence of the Russian accounts, but did not launch extensive investigations. Later I did inquire with them and was pretty surprised with the answer that I got: "Sharjah Branch audit was not in the plan this year."

I thought plans should be revised if circumstances warrant it and the auditors came later to investigate when we had already picked up the threads of the web. Following the trail, Abu Nasr had concluded some 17 banks and exchange houses in the UAE were part of this magical web. One particular bank account involved a turnover of many millions and Nasr was seen laughing because the customer's profession was a tour guide. Nasr remarked sarcastically that even guides are better off as they offer guidance on how to move funds. Our report recommended special investigation into these institutions, but Sultan looked the other way.

One interesting issue was a stupid query from the Governor inquiring about the sum involved in these accounts and we replied that the current balances in these accounts was around AED 100.00 million. He commented, "A very small sum," and we had to further educate him that these were the current balances in those accounts and did not include turnover in the accounts, the deposits and the subsequent substantial withdrawal of these deposits, leaving back a small balance. Further the bank had been closing a number of accounts from time to time, which were not reflected in the current balance.

A synopsis of some of the accounts is given below and HSBC later on quietly started closing them without reporting the closures to the Central Bank.

General Letter: MONEY LAUNDERING - RUSSIAN REVIEW (Hala TAHIR)

HSBC ⟨X⟩

General Letter
30Oct1999

Sent by: Hala TAHIR

To: George M SEQUEIRA/MGR OPS MEM/BBME/HSBC@HSBC
cc: Anita SURI/MGR NSC MEM/BBME/HSBC@HSBC
bcc:

From: Sima KAMELI Tel: 971 4 4041213
Our Ref: NSC DEP 991480   Your Ref:
Subject: MONEY LAUNDERING - RUSSIAN REVIEW

With reference to your Mail dated 19/10/99, and as you verbally advised we have performed a random check of the account documentation of those accounts with balances of AED200,000/- and above and give below the details:

(A) Majority of the accounts are non-resident accounts with no introducer. We cannot ascertain that an introducer was a must at the time of account opening as the rule for non-resisdent accounts have over the years changed to either introducer required or not.

(B) Account number of two brothers are 040-188021-211 and 040-035859-211. They are students sponsored by their father and have the same balance in their accounts which is AED 365,455.08.

(C) Account number 025-224734-130, balance AED 332,299.92 this is a joint account the husband is sponsored by Ateya Trading, he is working as a shop assistant and his salary is AED 3200/- and his wife is sponsored by him.

(D) Account Number 040-003196-050 balance AED 1,389,654.65 working at Voyage Trading Co Ltd, is holder of two passports with two different names. The old Passport name Mamedov Gamid and the new passport name Mammadov Hamid.

(E) Account Number 040-127458-001 is a current account holder. The letters of introduction provided by him states two different salary amounts - AED4000/- (old letter) and AED 3500/- + transportation + Acc. (new letter). He is working as a sales representative with Trio Trading Co. and his account balance is AED 307,296.62.

(F) Account Number 040-240293-130 balance of AED 1,799,258.34. Account holder is working for Maram Tourism & Cargo Co. as a clerk as mentioned in his residence visa and as a manager as mentioned in his account opening application. His monthly salary USD 5000/-

(G) Non-resident acount numbers 025-268137-130 balance AED 1,769,941.80 and account number 025-268129-130 balance AED

621,103.74 are both introduced by the same person Mr. Alexander Sutugin holder of account number 025-267691-130.

(H) Holder of account Number 025-206111-130 balance AED 965,703.45 is sponsored by Al Khaimah Perfumes Co. Her designation mentioned in the account opening form is 'business' and her monthly salary is USD 10,000

(I) Holder of account Number 040-072746 (AIG) has 11 different accounts with a total of AED 11,217,925.28 and is sponsored by Al Amal Enterprises.

We also would like to draw your attention to some of the following mentioned TMD accounts which have balances over AED One Million. However we are unable to provide any details as TMD documents are held at the branch :

A/C No. 025-118340-282	AED 1,156,558.17
A/C No. 025-121427-281	AED 1,190,263.53
A/C No. 025-157280-253	AED 1,398,637.59
A/C No. 025-157280-284	AED 1,801,493.86
A/C No. 020-390563-281	AED 1,101,070.55
A/C No. 025-002023-281	AED 2,170,262.81
A/C No. 025-044777-253	AED 1,821,223.52
A/C No. 025-063561-252	AED 2,069,433.04

Regards,

Sima Kameli
Deposit Executive

Memo: ML UPDATE (Chandrasekhar SWAMINATHAN)

HSBC ❎

Memo
14Mar2000

To: George M SEQUEIRA/MGR OPS MEM/BBME/HSBC@HSBC
cc: David W J BAGLEY/RLA LGA MEM/BBME/HSBC@HSBC
        John E COVERDALE/COC MEM/BBME/HSBC@HSBC
bcc:

From: Dilip HIREMATH   Tel: 971 6 5090235
Subject: ML UPDATE

PERSONAL ACCOUNTS

- During March, two accounts were closed, under non-profitable/ML suspicions. These accounts were of small balances and were of Russian nationals.

- We blocked 6 additional accounts of Russian/CIS nationality with high credit balances whom we are unable to contact. Letters are sent to them but these are not responded to yet. Nevertheless we will progress closure of these accounts immediately after the Eid holidays.

CORPORATE ACCOUNTS

Investigations are progressing to eliminate the suspicions on various accounts maintained with us. The following accounts are cleared from the suspicion list subsequent to meeting/discussions with the customer:

- Fu Net Trading Co LLC: A reply was submitted to George detailing the findings of our discussions with the customer. We may also be visiting their premises to reconfirm our findings.

- Shaikh Import N Export Co Ltd: Large transactions in the account demands a meeting with the customer. The concerned ARM will be enquiring the customer about his activity.

- Fortuna Used Cars: Similar to the above account, large cash transactions exist in this account. The business is owned by a Russian. Symptoms of ML will be investigated after meeting this customer soon after the Eid holidays.

The ML reports forwarded to us by George on 28 February 2000 are being investigated and our comments will be submitted as requested. In the meantime, we would be grateful if you could advise us the progress of the daily report split between PLB and CMB (with a possible subdivision by ARM's).

Regards

Dilip

THE AZERBAIJAN
BUSINESSMAN

A businessman opened a non-resident savings account denominated in US dollars, and as the file note indicates, substantial inward remittances were received in his account. In an interview, the businessman indicated that he was dealing in oil trades with Iran and Turkey but could not forward any documents to support his claim. Apparently no reasons were given as to why funds were being remitted from Turkey to UAE or the reasons for opening an account in HSBC Deira Dubai.

Incidentally the address in the bank's record was a post box in Baku, Azerbaijan. As good banking practice, inward remittances are credited to a depositor's account only when the bank is satisfied that such incoming funds commensurate with the depositors standings and his known status. The minute a bank credits the funds to a customer's account the bank has laundered the incoming funds and the outward remittance is a next step in the washing process to complete the cycle.

HSBC did not forward any Suspicious Activity Report to the Central Bank and would simply close the bank account and hand over the balance amount through a Cashiers Check. The Customer would simply go to another bank and on the strength of the Cashiers Check would easily open a bank account.

Ref No

SCHEDULE 2
HSBC GROUP

Form compiled Sept. '93

MONEY LAUNDERING SUSPICION REPORT

Please complete this form in as much detail as possible and return it to your relevant MLCO:

SOURCE:

Group Entity:	HSBC		
Office Address:	PO Box 66 DUBAI		
Your Name:	ANAND SHARMA		
Your Reference:		**Tel No:**	
Your Signature:		**Fax No:**	
Date of Report:	8 Jun 99		

SUSPICION:

Name of Account Holder:	HUSEYN ABBAS ABDULLAYEV		
Account No:	020 360 269 130	**Date of Birth:**	25 05 1967
Occupation:	Bussiness		
Address:	P.O Box 370000 BAKU - AZERBAJAN		

DETAILS OF SUSPICION:

Please provide details of suspicious transactions and other relevant data. Attach a separate sheet if necessary. (Include other suspects, nationality, etc. Attach copy IDs, transaction notes).

Huseyn A. Abdullayev an Azerbajan national opened a non-resident USD Savings Account with us on 3 Jan 1999. During March & April we have noticed extraordinary large volumes of inward remittances to his a/c (total USD 1.8 m) from Turkey. We have [illegible] the customer to call on us for an explanation regarding the large remittances. The customer called on us on 30 May 99 with his friend Mr Mustafa Safrini an interpretor of Russian language. Meeting took place in presence of Arun Nakre, Abraham [illegible], Bayan Emadi (who knows Russian) and the interpretor. Customer claims that he does Business in petrol and deals mainly with Turkey & Iran. But he had no documents with him to substantiate his claim. We have explained him that we do not allow personal customers to make their business transactions through the personal account and we may in due course ask him to supply us with the source of his funds for further explanation to UAE Central Bank. We have advised him to open a business a/c duly introduced by our Azerbajan office. Finally customer decided to close the a/c. We have allowed him to transfer the entire balance [illegible] back to his a/c in Turkey. We have close the a/c [illegible] transfer the balance to his a/c in Istanbul Turkey.

Other territories involved in the transaction:

Encl. Copy of Passport
Copy of Statement of account
Copy [illegible]

A Suspicious Activity Report which was not filed
with the Central Bank

FROM SWISS WITH LOVE: BITTER CHOCOLATES

If you eat too many creamy chocolates, it can raise your sugar levels, which can destroy your health. Although Swiss chocolates are pretty delicious, this one proved to be a poison pill to HSBC.

The Bank first credited large incoming funds to a customer, which did not match the customer's background and then the other enormous blunder was to debit his account without written authority and send the funds back to the country of origin - Switzerland in this case.

Sometimes technological inventions can backfire – HSBC's Hexagon System, which enables a customer to directly receive incoming funds into his account and also gives him the comfort of sitting in his home or office to transfer funds out using the internet based system without going to the bank and requesting an outward transfer was the primary villain in most of the cases.

However, this does not relieve the bank of its liability for not monitoring its accounts. Needless to say the bank did not furnish us the details on the account which I picked up during the examination. We do not know the customer's identity, or what constituted a large sum of money, or the outcome of the case.

HSBC Group Management, later adequately rewarded David Bagley's good work of hiding controversial cases from the regulators, and he was promoted from his post as the Head of Compliance in the Gulf Region to Head of Compliance for the HSBC Group in the UK.

My dear friends, read the facts as detailed in a memo sent by David Bagley to Abdul Jalil, Head of HSBC Middle East, and later forwarded to others staff for guidance.

The HSBC Group   MEMO

To   Distribution   12Jul1999
From   ABDUL JALIL YOUSUF BBME MEM   CEO Tel 971 4 5077309
Our Ref   Your Ref
Subject MONEY LAUNDERING SUSPICIOUS TRANSACTION

FYI.

Abdul Jalil Yousuf
Executive Director/CEO UAE

[Sent by BBME MEM CEO SEC(LOCAL)]

*********************** Forward Message ***************************

                                                                   MEMO
To   Distribution   12Jul1999
From   BAGLEY D W J BBME MEM LGA RLA Tel 971 4 5077697
Our Ref MEM LGA 991351   Your Ref
Subject MONEY LAUNDERING SUSPICIOUS TRANSACTION

In the spirit of ensuring that we as a bank learn from our
experience rather than out of a desire to embarrass anyone I have
set out below brief details of a recent case in one of our area
offices, giving details of the actions that were taken, the problems
that that has left us with, and my recommendations as to how, with
the benefit of hindsight, we should have best dealt with this
situation.

The Facts
=========

A large remittence in USD was received to the credit of an account
operated by an individual for which there was not history of any
similar transaction.

The monies were remitted in USD (a large round sum) from a small
Swiss bank via their and our US correspondents.

The monies were received and credited to the account by automatic
remittance, and subsequently the transaction was identified as being
an unusual large transaction warranting further investigation.

Having identified the transaction as unusual we sought confirmation
from the Swiss bank that the funds were "clean" and from a good
source.

The response of the Swiss bank was to indicate their intention to
request the return of the money, and whilst this was notified
verbally to our customer no authority or instruction was sought from
our customer.

Subsequently a tested message requesting the return of the funds on

                                                          .../2

Fraud case involving an unnamed Swiss Bank
shows the level of transparency followed at their Middle
Eastern operations.

- 2 -

the basis that they were "sent in error" was received from the Swiss bank, and against that tested request monies were debited to the account and returned to the Swiss bank.

The Bank has now received a claim from the customer requiring the return of these monies to him.

Whilst a request for the return of the funds has been passed back to the Swiss bank to date they have not responded.

Court proceedings have been commenced against the Bank by our disgruntled customer.

Relevant Additional Facts
==========================

Whilst there are local money laundering regulations these are limited to requiring the Bank to satisfy itself as to the true identity of customers but including no reporting or other requirements.

Our own existing KYC requirements are adequate to ensure compliance with this guidance.

Lesson To Be Learnt
===================

1.   There was probably little useful purpose served by asking the remitting bank to certify the source of funds.

      I would expect most banks to be reluctant to give any such certification, and further they would be bound by duties of confidentiality to their customer with whom we have no relationship.

2.   Our GPPs (which consist of a minimum standard of behaviour where GPPs impose a higher burden than local regulation) only require us to properly identify customers (KYC procedures) and to have a system for identifying and investigating suspicious transactions.

      The office dealing with this matter appear to have been motiviated in some of their actions by a feeling that they had some duties to protect public interest given that they were suspicious as to the true nature of source of the funds. Whilst this is laudable we are in no position to make such a judgement, nor do our GPPs impose any form of obligation in this regard.

3.   We should not have debited the customers account at the request of the remitting bank without instructions given in accordance with our mandate, or where we had a relevant court order or equivalent.

RUSSIAN MAFIA ATTACK OBAID'S HOUSE

On one Wednesday night, which is the weekend night in UAE, I was awakened by a call from Obaid telling me that his house in Sharjah was broken into by some criminals. He sounded pretty depressed and told me that the local police were examining his house for some clues. Interestingly no valuables were stolen but his new office briefcase was slashed with a knife. None of the working papers or files were with him as they were safely stored in Nasr's car.

The Police asked Obaid the nature of his job and, after listening to his replies, asked him to be on alert. He was told that this was the work of the Russian Mafia. Actually Obaid, who lived in Sharjah, had just returned from a party with his family and the attack was a warning not to cross their path or his life would be in danger.

Later I received a call from Nasr telling me about the attack at Obaid's house and he cautioned me to be on alert. Although both of us were already safely back in our homes in Abu Dhabi, some two and a half hours drive from Sharjah, but our hearts were with Obaid in Sharjah. None of us slept that night and kept calling each other at regular intervals the entire night. I don't think any one of us can forget that fateful Wednesday night and the memory of Obaid's helpless voice still haunts me.

As we were leaving for Sharjah in Nasr's car, after the frightful weekend, we were pretty scared and for the first time the music was switched on and we hardly talked during the ride. We decided to wrap up the audit as quickly as possible.

Nasr spoke to our manager about the whole episode on Thursday. The whole week we were nearly scared to death and our movements were restricted to leaving the hotel in the morning and returning back to the hotel in Sharjah.

I distinctly remember one of the HSBC staff casually asking Nasr at which hotel we were staying. Nasr gave me a scared look, but managed to keep the situation under control, saying only that during our audit we are forbidden to disclose our whereabouts. This is one of Nasr's qualities that he has a ready answer for even awkward questions.

Needless to say that Obaid hardly participated actively in the audit after that attack on his house. The dynamic Obaid we knew was now busy answering his mobile phone and assuring his callers that everything was well. He asked us what the Central Bank would do if somebody murdered us. His talk really made sense, and he told us that he would be searching for other employment.

Being a UAE citizen, switching jobs was very easy for him. He wanted to resign immediately but then somebody advised him to ask for premature retirement so that his current emoluments could continue for the rest of his life. A request for approval for early retirement was sent by him to the Governor, which was promptly denied.

We were pretty disappointed that his request for early retirement was not approved and not even a courtesy call was made by the Governor or Executive Director to Obaid inquiring about his well being. The overall morale and spirit of the team went down. God only knows how we completed the report and it was finally signed off at 10.00 pm on Wednesday. During the last week, we had put in a lot of extra time (no overtime is paid) as we did not want to spend any more time at HSBC. Obaid treated us to an excellent Arabic dinner and later Nasr and I went back to Abu Dhabi.

The report was submitted along with three boxes containing bank statements for controversial accounts to the Executive Director. Nasr also narrated the attack on Obaid's house.

WE WILL PUT
DAVID BAGLEY IN JAIL

Our report was lying somewhere in our department and nearly one month after its submission a one-page summary was forwarded by the Department. I am really ashamed to tell you that like most of the Government organizations, things move at a snail's pace at Central Bank.

On this memo, you can see the golden statement written by the Governor "If he said this, we can put him behind bars." After a week from the submission of this memo, a senior colleague informed me that the Governor wanted to see me with my team at exactly 2.00 pm to discuss the HSBC report. I immediately called Nasr and Obaid, and told them about the comment made by the Governor and added that a possible promotion was coming.

Nasr always used to comment that I am a very optimistic man, but that moment his voice was very hopeful and said "Insha Allah we will be promoted.". After all we had detected that HSBC one of the largest banks in Europe and second largest in the world has tons of skeletons in their closet and the keys to their treasured closet were in our hands.

Obaid was flying that afternoon for his vacation and hence could not attend the meeting but Nasr came immediately to the Central Bank. He was excited that for the first time in his life he would be meeting the Governor, after being in service for nearly two decades.

Time was not flying in the office that day and we were waiting for the appointment time to arrive. I remember Nasr took an hour off to go home and wear his best suit. After all, he was meeting the Governor for the first time. Believe me right up to 2 o'clock he was highly charged and was telling all and sundry in the Central Bank – I am meeting the Governor. He was very excited.

We were already on the fourth floor where the Governors office is located well before the scheduled time armed with our report and key working papers. Big guns of the department who had endorsed our report were also attending the meeting.

The Governor was perhaps in a very attacking mood and started criticizing our work based on the two-page memo forwarded to him by the department. The memo in all frankness did not give sufficient details but was only a brief summary. I inquired whether he read our report. To which he replied, "I have no time".

He then proceeded to make a columnar summary type of report and passed it to me with the comment, "fill this up and we meet later at 9.00 pm in the evening."

The whole afternoon both of us sat down and completed the columnar report by 6.00 in the evening and we then decided to go home. Nasr was pretty disappointed at the outcome of the meeting, and being a pessimist, was wondering what more bad news was coming next. He told me to tell my mother to pray for our well being and I relayed his message to my mother.

This time the clock struck 9 p.m. rather early, I thought. The columnar reports designed by him and duly filled in were passed on to the Governor. He looked at the first one and immediately crossed it and threw it on the table with a comment "Re-do it."

The second and the third met the same fate. The whole atmosphere was tense and no one from the department was saying anything.

I realized that all these big wigs at the department were paper tigers powerful only at the third floor, where Banking and Supervision is located. I had expected them to defend us; after all they had endorsed our report and forwarded a summary. The Governor angrily looked at me and said, "You are wasting my time."

All my life I have without any hesitation called a spade a spade and basically I don't take nonsense from anybody.

I immediately replied that it was impossible to give detailed information in a columnar report and pointed out the Bank statements covering those controversial accounts. The memo of David Bagley, addressed to the Groups Compliance Manager in the UK, stating they were involved in laundering but will not report it to the UAE Central Bank, was passed on to the Governor. He inquired whether we had bank statements covering these accounts. I pointed to a bundle of statements, which were kept on the table and commented that 3 boxes more are with the department.

The Governor very reluctantly picked one of them. As he saw the first bank statement he picked up his pencil and started circling large amounts coming in and going out. I then passed him another statement and his eyes popped out in surprise. Executive Director then said, "Please pass him more statements." At this point, Abu Nasr got a boost of courage and picked up two more statements and started explaining to him in Arabic.

Now, Abu Nasr informed the Governor about the attack on Obaid's home and about the Deira branch Manager's proposal to introduce Russian girls to us. The Governor pushed his chair back and said call David Bagley tomorrow at 10.00 in the morning to meet us. Abu Nasr immediately spoke to Bagley on his mobile phone.

As we were leaving for home, Abu Nasr said, "It seems your mom's prayers have worked for us." We were excited that tomorrow David Bagley would be arrested, as the Governor had written on the memo that we would put him in jail.

Bagley called me up to inquire whether any files were required for his visit so that he could carry from his office in Dubai, but I told him we had sufficient input and wished him a safe trip. At the appointed hour everybody was present on the fourth floor meeting room.

I shudder to think what must have been in Bagley's mind when he drove, but I can definitely tell you that his return trip back to his office must have been hell. He will probably remember it for the rest of his life. The driving time between Abu Dhabi and Dubai is roughly around ninety minutes and I hope Bagley took the bank's car and the driver, because after the hammering the Governor gave him, it would be a big task to drive back to Dubai, given the frame of mind he was in after the meeting.

Both Abu Nasr and I were in top gear that morning but decided that we would leave the court to the Governor and we were certainly not disappointed. He began, "My boys did a wonderful job, because from your office they have picked your memo addressed to your London bosses wherein you have mentioned that you have laundered funds here in UAE, but will not tell the UAE Central Bank because there is no law on money laundering in the UAE."

Abu Nasr picked up a copy of the memo and passed it to Bagley. The meaning of my surname or family name is "Doctor" as my forefathers were into that profession and although I do not know anything about medicine, surely I can vouch that Bagley is a healthy man, because any other person would have had a stroke.

Bagley's face turned pale and he fell speechless, mumbling apologies. The Governor like a lion started to roar and said that "You launder funds and the Russian mafia attacks my boys and that Deira Manager offers Russian girls to my auditors."

We were now expecting that the Governor would call up the security and get him arrested. Bagley then mentioned that their Group Chairman Bond was recently in town and was fully aware of the laundering episode. The Governor asked Bagley to leave and right up to the door, he was apologizing.

Inter-Office Memorandum

To   :   Governor's Office
From   :   Banking Supervision and Examination Department
Date   :   8th June 2000
Ref. No. : 13/14 8 2 /2000
Subject :   Accounts of Russian Nationals at UAE Branches of
            HSBC Bank Middle East – Money Laundering

===

It has been noticed by our examiners that the branches of HSBC Bank Middle East, UAE have been very active in opening of accounts of Russian customers.

I do not are about the bank definition.

HSBC's definition of Russian Customers include customers from any of the states of the former Soviet Union, now the Commonwealth of Independent States (CIS) plus customers from the Baltic Countries viz Estonia, Latvia and Lithuania.

Most of the accounts are at their Deira and Sharjah branches. Total number of Russian accounts at the Bank's branches in the UAE is 1,186 with a deposit base of AED 125.3 Mln.

Review of accounts at the Bank's Sharjah and Deira branches were carried out by our examiners. Bank Statements of all the Russian accounts for the last two years were examined. Their turnover details are indicative of money laundering on a massive scale. The management of the Bank at Sharjah and Deira branches failed to observe their internal policy guidelines with regard to "Know Your Customer (KYC)" and review of the daily large transactions report. At the Bank's Deira branch, one of the staff was of Russian nationality designated to deal with Russian clients. According to our examiners, activities at the Bank's Sharjah branch in particular is a cause of concern.

Our examiners have also observed that incoming remittances in some of the accounts did not commensurate with the level of disclosed income.

If he said this call him to see me.

HSBC Bank Middle East Compliance Officer/Legal Advisor, Mr. David Bagley has acknowledged that the Bank is guilty of money laundering in the case of Semenchenko Group at Sharjah branch. He has, however, taken a view that in the absence of a law on money laundering in the UAE, the Bank is under no legal compulsion to inform the Central Bank of the UAE. Mr. Saeed Al Jaberi, an executive of the Bank's Sharjah branch had links with Semenchenko Group. He has been dismissed from the Bank's service.

We can put him in prison.

It may be mentioned here that Semenchenko Group has as account with ABN-Amro Bank and the Group had once maintained a relationship with MashreqBank also. Semenchenko Group's accounts at HSBC Bank Middle East's Sharjeh branch is now on the exit list. It has also been reported that Semenchenko Group has dealings with Thomas Cook Al Rostamani Exchange Company.

Contd..2

Memo dated June 8, 2000 signed by Saeed was forwarded to Suwedi, who commented on Bagley – call him to see me. We can put him in prison. Sultan did not follow his words with actions – a sign that empty weapons make more noise.

/.

Conclusion

The Bank is not following our instructions contained in the Circular No. 163/98 dated 28/02/1998 concerning unusual transactions in an account. They did not report to the Central Bank details of such accounts involving dubious transactions. They also quietly closed some accounts involving money laundering and did not report them to the Central Bank.

Our examiners are of the view that we should write to the Bank expressing seriousness of the matter and our concern in this regard.

Submitted for H.E. the Governor's information and instructions.

Approved .... موافق
*Detailed analysis of each of
every account (in doubt) should
be given to me first.*

11/06/2000

com:/mt/hsbcrusacctgo.edmi

CALL FSA AND RAID HSBC MIDDLE EAST

After the meeting, the Governor was in full elements and instructed Saeed to:

- Call Financial Service Authority (FSA are the regulators for UK banks and for foreign banks operating in the UK) people in London and tell them to come to UAE immediately, tell them to catch the first plane and travel all night.
- Send twenty examiners to HSBC from tomorrow
- Call the head of HSBC in Dubai to terminate the Manager and Operation Manager of HSBC Sharjah and the Branch Manager of HSBC Deira.

At this point, I interrupted the Governor and said "Why FSA? Are we not good enough as examiners?" To which he replied that he had to involve them as a protocol.

The Executive Director immediately called Abdul Jalil Darwish, the Head of HSBC Dubai, and conveyed the

Governor's decision to terminate the three persons involved. It is a pity that the Governors decision was not implemented by HSBC and the officers involved are still employed and merrily enjoying.

The FSA did arrive and met the Governor and HSBC Management. However, this I understand was strictly a closed-door meeting with the Governor and the Executive Director and few others. One of the reviewer's at the department explained to me later that FSA was giving the Governor a very hard time and was threatening to close the UAE local banks operating in London on the grounds that UAE is a high risk country with regards to money laundering. By exposing HSBC you gave a golden opportunity to the Governor to twist the ears of FSA and tell them what your UK Bank was doing in UAE.

I immediately remembered one top official of a local bank having a branch in London complaining to me about the constant problems they were facing with FSA. I am sure I don't have to tell readers what arrangements were negotiated with FSA, but I would like to tell you that at the next meeting of Financial Action Task Force (FATF), UAE was not in the money laundering black list. The UAE Delegation to this FATF, among others, included Abdullah Muhairy (one of the twenty examiners who went with me to HSBC later) and the delegation members were jubilant.

After he came back, he told me that he had asked the Head of the anti-money-laundering unit at the Central Bank whether this was because we had a lot of evidence against HSBC, and the answer was "yes."

Abdullah Muhairy is a young UAE national and has a soft spot for me and every time tells me that when he becomes the Governor, he will definitely remember to promote me.

I would like to add further that the Federal Reserve of USA were never intimated by the UAE Central Bank, although the incoming and outgoing remittances were mostly in US dollars and were routed through HSBC New York. I have every reason to believe that HSBC, which in the end escaped freely without paying a single dollar as fine or penalty in the UAE, would have been in big trouble in USA.

However, my belief turned wrong and despite forwarding documentary evidence to Bank Regulators in the US and the UK the big fish got away. The reviewer also told me that our team's recommendation to impose fines on HSBC would not hold any water because the UAE law does not have a provision whereby the Central Bank could impose fines or penalties on banks violating the law. I think it is high time that a change is necessary.

To show his importance, the Governor now sent a team of 20 examiners to HSBC's UAE Branches, telling me and Abu Nasr not to inform the other 18 members of the team of the reason for the raid on HSBC. The rest of the team were sent on a wild goose chase to review general banking operations and had absolutely no clue about the whole mission.

One western examiner ran into a stunningly beautiful Managress and wanted to date her, but was rebuked badly. One of the team members informed me and I had to apologize to her and to Coverdale. A complaint was launched with the Executive Director but no action was taken noting his white skin and blue eyes.

HSBC's management also started playing games. Key people were simultaneously transferred immediately, the most prominent being Coverdale and Phillips Dawe. Both were given excellent new assignments so as to shut their mouths forever.

Most importantly they were out of the scene and we had to deal with their successors transferred from HSBC's other overseas branches. To make matters worse, a young summer trainee was given the responsibility of coordinating with us and this adversely impacted our work.

During our 10-day investigation, some 20-odd memos were sent to the Governor and our department but no response was received. One morning a new simultaneous assignment was given to me and Abu Nasr regarding the "Congo Promissory Note Fraud" and we were running from one bank to another while the rest of the team ran aimlessly on an unknown mission.

One of the reviewers from the UK who was not given access to the examination report as a deliberate ploy by the management, was heard saying, "This Kamikaze style raid is politically motivated and poor HSBC, being a British Bank, is being victimized." I am sure after reading my bible on HSBC my friend will eat his words.

Fax ed. 12/6

CENTRAL BANK OF THE U.A.E.

مصرف الإمارات العربية المتحدة المركزي

Date : 12/ 6 /2000

Ref : 13-2/87/2000

التاريخ : 18 / ٦ / ٢٠٠٠

الإشارة : ١٣–٢/٨٧/٢٠٠٠

Mr. Abdul Jalil Yousuf Darwish
Executive Director &
Chief Executive Officer (U.A.E.)
HSBC Bank Middle East
P. O. Box 66
Dubai

السيد/عبدالجليل يوسف درويش   المحترم
عضو مجلس الإدارة التنفيذي
والمسؤول التنفيذي الرئيسي (أ.ع.م.)
بنك اتش.اس.بي.سي، الشرق الأوسط
ص. ب : ٦٦
ديـــــبـــــي

After greeting,

السلام عليكم ورحمة الله وبركاته،

This is to advise you that Messrs. Iqbal Hakim, Sultan Ali Jassim, Gary Waple, Thomas Dodd, Robert Clarke, Nigel Morgan, Anthony Wilson, Issa Shuker, Abou Al Nasr Youssef, Ahmad Fadly, Martin Williams, Anthony Day, Rupert Evans, Abdullah Al Muhairi, Mabrouk H. Mabrouk, I. Abdel Fadil, Adel Al Sayyegh, Nasser Al Sayyah, Jens Klinzing, Akbar Muhajir, John Hindly and Alain Jean Bernard from the Banking Supervision & Examination Department will be visiting your Bank for a special examination.

يرجـــــى التكـــــرم بالعلـــــم أن السـادة/إقبال حكيم، سلطان علي جاسـم، غاري وابل، توماس دود، روبرت كـلارك، نايجل مورغن، انتوني ويلسـون، عيسـى شكر، أبو النصر يوسـف، احمـد فضلـي، مارتن ويليامز، انتوني داي، روبرت ايفنز، عبدالله المهيري، مـبروك حمـد مـبروك، ابراهيم عبدالفضيل، عادل الصايغ، نـاصر الصياح، جنز كلينزينغ، اكبر مهاجر، جـون هندلي والين جين برنارد مــــن دائــــرة الرقابة والتفتيش علـــى المصــــارف سيقومون بزيارة بنككم يـوم ٢، ٣ لإجراء تفتيـش خاص.

We shall appreciate your co-operation in this regard.

وسـوف نقدر لكم تعاونكم بهـذا الخصــوص .

Yours Faithfully,

وتفضلوا بقبول فائق الاحترام ،

سعيد عبدالله الحامز
المديــر التنفيذي
لدائرة الرقابة والتفتيش على المصارف
Saeed Abdulla Al Hamiz
Executive Director
Banking Supervision & Examination Department

SH/ak
My doc/BSED/Exam/fb/S-hsbc4

ابو ظبي - ص.ب: ٨٥٤، تلفون: ٦٥٢٢٢٠، فاكس: ٦٥٢٥٠٤ (٠٢) - تلكس: الادارة العامة / العمليات المصرفية: ٢٢٣٩٦ / ٢٢٥٧٧ - الخزانة: ٢٢٣٣٠ / ٢٣٣١٦ - مراقبة الفروع دبي: ٥٣٦٥٥٠
ABU DHABI - P.O.Box: 854 - Telephone: 652220 - Fax: (02) 652504 - Tlx.: Management / Banking Operations 22396 / 22577, Treasury: 22330 / 23316
Branches Telephones: Dubai: 536655, SHJ: 592592, RAK: 223330, Al Ain: 656656, FUJ: 224040 - الشارقة: ٥٩٢٥٩٢، رأس الخيمة: ٢٢٣٣٣٠، العين: ٦٥٦٦٥٦، الفجيرة: ٢٢٤٠٤٠ - دبي: ٠١-٢٢٤

A team of 20 Examiners raiding HSBC Middle East Bank's branches.

ARMS BAZAAR OF ABU DHABI & VICTOR BOUT - THE MERCHANT OF DEATH

The annual International Defense Exhibition (IDEX in Abu Dhabi) is a market where arms merchants, brokers, and middlemen from all over the world flock in big numbers duly supported by their respective governments, have been royally milking the oil countries of the Middle East, over the last two decades. At IDEX, one could buy the latest weapons from small arms to tanks, patriot missiles, helicopters, fighter aircraft, and submarines, and yes, the popular AK-47.

I understand that the inventor of the Kalashnikov AK-47, Mikhail Kalashnikov, was also once present in IDEX, to boost the sale of his dream destruction weapon, which is a favorite with terrorists all over the world. The devil had himself come all the way to show his craft to the audience.

The Middle East is the largest arms market accounting for around 40% of the international arms trade. It is reported that during 1987-97 Saudi Arabia alone spent a total of $262 billion on strengthening its military, most of which is from the US & Europe.

I am told that buying weapons at IDEX is as simple as buying groceries from your local supermarket and is a billion dollar industry. Combat Films & Research for the Kennedy Center has produced a film titled "Arms Bazaar" based on IDEX to highlight the dangers of selling so many arms.

International observers have noted that many weapons purchased legally by a country turn up being used for illicit purposes in another, and although the International Network on Small Arms (IANSA) and other such organizations are working to address the proliferation and misuse of arms, their efforts remain largely unsuccessful. Following Saddam Hussein's capture, the world has seen that arms and ammunition sold by the western countries are used against their soldiers in Iraq.

The dangerous arms market combined with the reluctance of the UAE Authorities to take measures against arms and nuclear brokers further complicates the plot. One of the arms merchants is Victor Bout and the other, an associate of the disgraced atomic scientist.

Victor Bout, a Russian arms dealer, had an important base in Sharjah, popularly referred to as the Merchant of Death, his companies and associates were banking with HSBC Sharjah branch. HSBC's Internal Audit report indicates that their controversial employee, Saeed Al Jabri was very close to the group and had borrowed lots of money from them.

Bout has been indicted in Belgium on money laundering charges and UN enforcement officials have found that his airline, San Air, and other companies were involved in shipping weapons to Charles Taylor, the former controversial President of Liberia. Reports indicate that Bout had a fleet of 50 airplanes parked at Sharjah and used for transporting arms and ammunition into Angola, Rwanda, Sierra Leone and the Congo.

Bout, a shrewd operator, never took chances and conducted business using front men. International investigators believe Bout sold arms and in settlement obtained diamonds from the rebel groups in Africa. Such diamonds are also referred to as blood diamonds or conflict diamonds.

Bout had no difficulty in converting the blood diamonds into hard cash in the notorious gold and diamond Souk of UAE without any questions asked. The UN believes that illicit diamond trading is fueling wars in Africa and is being used as a conduit for terrorist financing.

One of its directives to the World Diamond Council is to tackle the issue and ensure that all diamond merchants are able to provide guarantees on the origin of all diamonds traded by them certifying that the diamonds are conflict free. The phrase "conflict-free diamond" is a foreign language to diamond dealers in the UAE.

I had traced various bank accounts related to Bout at another UK bank, following an article in the Financial Times on his arms dealings, which were a cause of concern to the UK and US authorities. I had recommended to Suweidi to block these funds but he came back asking for three good reasons and I promptly gave him six, but still he did not freeze those accounts and came back strongly saying that UAE being an independent country does not take orders from the UK and USA.

This incident happened well before 9/11. Salim, a charming reviewer who actually would prosper more in Hollywood, came back and said, "Six good reasons and what more could you need?" Salim is a highly qualified British citizen and another victim of discrimination, because of his subcontinent origin. Thus Victor Bout was allowed a free hand to run his operations.

Some years back I had classified an exposure as a bad one at a top Abu Dhabi bank and surprisingly the bank management did not raise their voice when I requested them to make a 100% provision for this delinquent loan. The $5 million loan was advanced to a company, which was run by a front man for a Very Important Person (VIP) and was involved in making bullets at their factory.

AN EX-US GENERAL & THE ATOMIC KHAN CONNECTION

In February 2002, an examiner picked up a conversation in a bar that a company, Emirates Palomar Medical Technology Service (EPMTS) based in Abu Dhabi had gone down and owed millions and millions of dollars to creditors, including some six months of unpaid wages to the staff. I was asked to review the case and the bank refused to hand over the main file, claiming that it was a sensitive defense contract. Based on the shadow file it was observed that EPMTS was a special purpose limited liability company set up to assist the UAE Government in upgrading the medical services and healthcare capabilities of its Armed Forces.

As per bank files, the company was 51% owned by a UAE company (using a front man) and 49% owned by a US company, incorporated in North Carolina, USA, called Eagle Technologies, Inc., and reportedly owned by Buster C. Glosson and Rick D Cantwell , both American citizens.

Their records indicated that the project was run by a former US General, a veteran of the Kuwait-related Gulf war.

Glen Simpson of the Wall Street Journal immediately identified Buster as the ex-General and was eager to expose him. It is a mystery why he kept quiet, but maybe some influential people somewhere held the remote control. I believe ex-generals working or doing business with foreign entities is a dangerous proposition, and the US Government should review this seriously.

EPMTS had signed a huge contract of USD $2.856 Billion with GHQ UAE Armed Forces, spread over a period of 14 years (it is to be noted that the contract was directly awarded and was not subject to any public bidding/tender). The payment of the contract was under LC established by the Finance Department and the contract proceeds were payable in quarterly payments of USD $51 million over 56 quarters.

In accordance with the contract, EPMTS received the 6th quarter payment in July 2001 and on 29th September 2001, GHQ cancelled the contract. As per bank file, the company's operating performance was adversely impacted by the dispute between the partners. Later, we heard that the Government of Abu Dhabi had all of a sudden cancelled the contract and had stepped in and taken over the company's liabilities.

I approached the Governor and he indicated that he would personally follow the case. Even to this day I cannot understand how the General who was not a doctor could run this "medical project" – I mean zero medical background and executing a near USD $3 billion project running for 14 years, and now with the deadly Nuclear Khan connection in UAE confirmed, I wonder whether this really was a medical contract or camouflaged?

Recently, in April, 2004 when a Sri Lankan businessman based in Dubai was accused by the US of brokering black market deals for nuclear technology,

Suweidi did not take action immediately, but much later very reluctantly froze the accounts concerned when the US came down heavily on this broker connected to the disgraced nuclear scientist – Nuclear Khan as I call him. President Bush has called this person the nuclear network's "Chief Financial Officer and Money launderer."

I am sure if this was known before 9/11, nothing would have happened and the businessman would still be making hay like Victor Bout, who was deported to Russia from UAE after 9/11, when all eyes were on him.

Incidentally Bout is an extraordinarily powerful person and is sheltered by influential people in Russia who will not hand him over to the UN and simply deny his existence in Russia.

The annual arms bazaar, Victor Bout, the US General link and the Atomic Khan's connection, coupled with the fact that the country gives sanctuary to dreaded gangsters (who are known as respected businessman in the community), ignores warnings from the rest of the world and allows arms dealers and launderers to operate freely, makes UAE a dangerous country for world peace effort.

The Indian Government will vouch for this and had Bal Thackeray (the leader of Shiv Sena Party of India) been the Prime Minister of India, they would have attacked UAE to flush out the criminals sitting in Dubai who had launched a series of bomb blasts in the Indian trading city of Mumbai (formerly called Bombay). The Indian Government's repeated pleas to hand over the criminals living in UAE went unheard. The whole world supported the US after 9/11 for the war on terror, which should have been started after terrorists struck my birthplace, Mumbai, in a deadly attack killing thousands of innocent people.

Unfortunately, India did not get any support. While there are terror attacks everywhere in the world, none of them has happened on UAE soil partly because it has been home for people with questionable backgrounds who own flourishing businesses in the UAE, which they would not like to be destroyed or disrupted by such attacks.

A file picture showing a car converted into an airplane stands on the corniche of Abu Dhabi – Thank God it cannot fly to the US.

BANKER TO A US SENATOR

Banks generally hesitate to open accounts for politicians and other diplomatic persons or foreign leaders, as later on the bank might become involved in a controversy connected to such a customer. Nevertheless there are no laws that prohibit banks from opening accounts for political figures, their relatives, family members or close associates, but enhanced scrutiny is to be performed to ascertain the source of funds in their accounts.

Riggs Bank in the US was recently fined a record $25 million by regulators for failing to report questionable financial transactions involving foreign customers including the governments of Equatorial Guinea and Saudi Arabia.

Maintaining bank accounts for foreign governments are a high risk and therefore most of the banks and are not at all interested in maintaining bank accounts for embassy clients. Riggs Bank decided to exit the Embassy banking business, but HSBC has stepped in to target Embassy accounts by opening a branch in Washington. By the end of

2004, some $1 billion Embassy-related deposits from Riggs are up for grabs.

I was surprised to read that Riggs Bank, which is exiting its lucrative bread and butter segment, is working closely with HSBC to take over its Embassy portfolio after being stabbed in the back by HSBC. As the story goes Riggs Bank had transferred funds from the US to HSBC Group entities in Cyprus and Luxembourg for the benefit of some customers and when Riggs and the US Banking Authorities demanded HSBC disclose the identities and ownership details, the reply came, "Sorry. Confidentiality rules."

So while Riggs faced the fines, HSBC got away laughing and the US Regulators cut a sorry figure because they do not have any claws and teeth on other sovereign countries, Cyprus and Luxembourg in this case. HSBC used the same weapon when I demanded that the UAE management forward us a list of accounts being investigated by US regulators maintained by HSBC Bank Middle East in the UAE and receiving substantial remittances from US.

I give below a classic example of HSBC Middle East overlooking the basic rules of banking, and would like to educate them that when funds are dumped on the counter, the bank should transfer such funds to a suspense account and immediately inform the Regulators and lodge a complaint with the local police, because the funds dumped could be proceeds of a criminal act. Let's see what fines are imposed by helpless US Regulators on this one, but HSBC has the right people at the right places.

SCHEDULE 2
Ref No   HSBC GROUP   Form compiled Sept.'93

MONEY LAUNDERING SUSPICION REPORT

Please complete this form in as much detail as possible and return it to your relevant MLCO:

SOURCE

Group Entity	HSBC Bank Middle East		
Office Address	Deira Branch, Nasr Square, Deira, Dubai, UAE		
Your Name	Mohd A Amiri		
Your Reference		Tel. No.	04-2074225
Your Signature		Fax No.	04-249490
Date of Report	19JUN99		

SUSPICION

Name of Account Holder	James Grant	
Account No.	025-255941-130	Date of Birth :
Occupation	Ex-Congressman / Businessman	
Address	932 Summerbrooke Drive, Tallahassee, FL 32312, USA	

DETAILS OF SUSPICION :   *A/c expand borrows / Halaments from inception*

Please provide details of suspicious transactions and other relevant data. Attach a separate sheet if necessary. (Include other suspects, nationality, etc. Attach copy Ids, transaction notes).

Mr. Grant approached the Bank to open a non-resident USD Savings A/c on 04APE99. I personally interviewed him and he had informed us that he would be receiving funds from abroad, especially Somalia. It was explained to him that no large transactions (cash/transfers) would be allowed. He subsequently credited his account with AED1.2 million cash through a third party who dumped the money at the counter and refused to take it back. Therefore we had no alternative but to accept the cash and block the account. Mr. Grant was called for an interview with myself and the circumstances were explained to him for closure of the account. The Account was closed on 28APR99.

Note: Mr. Grant claims to be doing business with people in Somalia dealing in recycling paper and since there is no banking facility there, the business dealings are done by cash.

Other territories involved in the transaction

Suspicious Activity Report not filed with the UAE Central Bank, but picked up by Auditors during the examination. The account-holder's occupation is listed as ex-congressman and business man, with an address in the U.S.

VIOLATION OF US/UN SANCTIONS

During the examination, we ran into a company owned by a Sudanese dealing in oil and were surprised that instead of doing business through letters of credit (LC's), large inward transfers and cash were used. Oil is purchased customarily by irrevocable confirmed LC's, but in this case tons and tons of hard cash was used instead. At HSBC's regional office, a smart Indian chap is employed who was nicknamed by me as a Cover Up man. It was his job to cover all irregularities. When this case was picked up, the coverman's reply is given below.

Timothy Brian, another high ranking reporter from the New York Times and considered to be an expert on Middle East matters was recommended by someone. Tim, like his reporter clan, was pressing day in and day out to meet me and on reading the name of Warm Seas Development nodded his head in excitement and, like Glen Simpson of the Wall Street Journal, promised to come out with an article.

However, reporters like politicians believe in the maxim that promises are meant to be broken. All they want from you is your reports and documents and my sincere advice to the world is not to trust them. After all they are an integral party of this corrupt world and hence I had decided to take the lead and self-publish my story.

I had heard a lot of stories of mafia being involved in dealing with stolen oil, and tankers being hijacked by pirates. In UAE banking circles, buying oil through hard cash was unheard of and I had approached the head of HSBC Trade Finance who had confirmed that oil is financed strictly through irrevocable letters of credit opened by a first class international bank and duly confirmed by a UAE Bank.

I don't know what penalties will be imposed by the US/UN Authorities on this one, but I know that HSBC has more power than the combined net of the US and the UN.

27/03/2000 14:26:36 (George M SEQUEIRA)

Memo
27Mar2000

To:　　David W J BAGLEY/RLA LGA MEM/BBME/HSBC
cc:　　John E COVERDALE/COO MEM/BBME/HSBC
　　　Phillip A DAWE/MGR GAM MEM/BBME/HSBC
bcc:

Subject:　GENERAL AUDIT -HBME FUJAIRAH

David,

I refer to Section 4.1 of the above report.

M.K.International (FZE)

This is a sole proprietorship owned by Mutasim Abdulla Kanoon, a sudanese National.The company was established in the Sharjah Free Trade Zone in Aug99 to conduct oil related trading activities.Mutasim started this company after a dispute with his cousin Abdulla Zaroug(owner of Warm Seas) .

Inward remittances are predominantly received from ENOC through the National Bank of Dubai and from Bakri Trading (large company based in Sharjah) through the Riyadh Bank,Riyadh.

Cash payments have been sometimes made to purchase oil directly from the tankers crew to benefit from discounts.Oil is sold to ENOC ,EPPCO,FAL and Bakri Trading.

Documentary Credits have been opened in favour of M.K. International by International Banks in India (ANZ Gridlays Bank , Mumbai) .Export Bills were discounted by the branch. On occasion part of the value of the DCs have been transferred to ENOC as the second beneficiary.

There has been some concern on whether or not the oil has been purchased from a legitimate source.There is documentary evidence that the oil has been purchased from the Iranian Oil terminal but no evidence as to the legitimacy of the ultimate source.Documents required under the DC included a Quality acceptance Report issued by an by an independent surveyor of international repute.SGS India LTD issued this report.

The business is profitable but we run a reputational risk groupwide if the US/UN authorities believe that we ought to have been aware that sanctions were overlooked. On the other hand in the absence of concrete evidence we could attract adverse publicity(due to the nature of the M.K.s customers) by attempting to exit the relationship.

In respect of providing bunkering services Fujairah is one of the largest ports in the world. Many operators (financed by other banks) therefore engage in a similar and related business. An exit without proper investigation into the environment and the working of the trade will also attract bad publicity in the market.

I intend raising a suspicion report for circulation only within MEM (not copied to the branch as this fact could reach the customer) and will monitor the large transactions for a period of two months before a decision is made.During these two months we will need to ascertain/validate:

1. The mechanism of booking quotas in advance at the Val Fajer Terminal 2 (Hormuz Strait). Briefly through this system a position of the forward price of oil is taken.Once the quota is confirmed payment is expected to be made immediately.Cash is apparently withdrawn to pay the exchange houses who undertake immediate settlement of the deals.

...000 14:26:36 (George M SEQUEIRA)

2. The mechanism by which the oil for food embargo is administered. For example can this approved quota be sold in the spot market?

Warm Seas Development

Incorporated in Sharjah and owned by a Sudanese, Abdulla Zarroug. Zarroug is of Sudanese origin and is now a Canadian national and one who has received formal education in the US/Canada.

We have received a good status report from Credit Suisse(Private Banking) who maintain the principal office account (Warm Seas Interanational Group). Warm Seas Group annual business is about USD 150 million and DCs are opened regularly with Credit Suisse.

Internal remittances are predominantly received from Greece,US and Europe.These payments are initiated either by companies involved in the shipping business or from Warm Seas group.

I do not recommend that an MLSR is raised for this account but the activities of the account will be placed on a watch list.

Kind regards,

George

BANKER TO TERRORIST ORGANIZATIONS

Post 9/11, the US authorities issued list of terrorist organizations, and banks all over the world were asked to identify and freeze bank accounts connected with terrorists.

HSBC UAE Branches have admitted that they do maintain bank accounts for such terrorist organizations. It is rather surprising that despite our criticism, the Know Your Customer (KYC) policy is still not being strictly implemented. HSBC staff is more concerned at opening new bank accounts to take advantage of the incentive policy associated with booking new clients at the Bank.

As seen below, the balances are pretty large and one would be interested to know the turnover and detailed transactions flowing through such accounts.

Sultan who was increasingly turning a blind eye on HSBC's Middle East operations did not allow us to review these accounts, which would have given us some trail on the remitters and end beneficiaries.

Based on the scarce information provided by them, the inward transfers originated from Al Baraka Exchange in Oslo and Brakat Exchange in Vancouver, and carried messages like "Help for Somalia" , "Aid for Somalia", and "Support for Somalians." HSBC reported these accounts only when the US authorities were on the lookout for terrorist related accounts and did not volunteer to inform the Central Bank despite being aware of the above disturbing messages accompanying the inward remittances.

Following the 9/11 attack on America, President Bush had issued an Executive Order freezing the assets of individuals and organizations that support terrorism. Al Baraka Group, owned by Somalis and having major operations in Dubai, was accused of transferring profits and interest to Al Qaeda. The US Authorities seized funds belonging to the group under the new Patriot Act.

US investigators believe that Barakat, a financial and telecommunications conglomerate operating in many countries around the globe, has pumped millions and millions of dollars to Osama bin Laden's Al Qaeda organization. Paul O'Neil, the US Treasury secretary, nicknamed the group as a "Hawala Conglomerate".

I understand US authorities had raided Al Baraka Exchange and forced the Central Bank to close this entity immediately.

In my opinion, the UAE Central Bank must be pressured to allow international investigators unhindered access to conduct a post mortem of such accounts, so as to pierce the veil of persons hiding behind these accounts and prosecute them.

11-81 16:85 MEM OPERATIONS DUBAI   ID=00971 4 3538728   P.01

Mr Saeed Abdulla A -Hamiz
Executive Director
Banking Supervisio: & Examination Department
Central Bank of the :AE
P O Box 854
Abu Dhabi   November 11, 2001

Ref: UAE COO 01C 02

Dear Mr Saeed,

CENTRAL BANK NOTICE NO. 2/351/01 DATED 07NOV01

Further to our fax n :ssage dated 08NOV01, sent under reference no. MEM BOP 010269 to the
Manager Special Un it of Banking Supervision and Examination department, we wish to advise
you that we have su sequently identified an account in the name of Barako Trading Company.

This account may l : related to the entities listed as "Entities assisted terrorists" in the above
notice for the follo\ ng reasons:

1. The account nan e carries the address of "P O Box 3313, Dubai";
2. Inward payment nave been received from al Baraka Exchange I Mn'
3. Inward payment have been received from Brakat Exchange Ltd., Vancouver;
4. The payment de ails on some inward messages received from Al Baraka Exchange carried
   the narratives "l elp for Somalia", "Aid for Somalia" and "Support for Somalians".

We would be grate: il if you could advise us urgently, by return fax (04-3538728), whether the
above funds related o the accounts of the above entity should be frozen.

Yours sincerely,
for HSBC Bank Mi die East

Steve Freeman
Chief Operating Of cer

HSBC Bank Middle Ea t   بنك إقتل إمو مي سي الشرق الأوسط
Middle East Managemc t Office   مكتب . إدارة فشرق الأوسط
PO Box 66, Dubai, Unit d Arab Emirates   ص.ب . ٦٦ ، دبي، الإمارات العربية المتحدة
Tel: 971-4-3535000 Fax: 71-4-3531005   هاتف ... ٩٧١.٤.٣٥٣٠... فاكس ٩٧١.٤.٣٥٣١...
Telex: 45424 HSBCD EM T legrams: Bactria Dubai   تلكس HSBCD EM ٤٥٤٢٤ برقياً : باكتريا دبي
Web: www.hsbc.com   Web: www.hsbc.com
Incorporated in England by Re al Charter 1889   تأسست في إنجلترا بموجب ميثاق ملكي عام ١٨٨٩
with limited liability   بمسئولية محدودة

11/11 '01 SUN 16:30 [TX/RX NO 6901] @001

The Manager, Special Unit
Banking Supervision & Examination Department
Central Bank of the UAE
P O Box 854
Abu Dhabi

Date: 12 November, 2001

Our reference : MEM BOP 010274

Dear Sir,

Re: CENTRAL BANK NOTICE NO. 2/351/01 DATED 07NOV01

Further to our fax messages reference MEM BOP 010269 dated 08NOV01 and UAE COO 010102 dated 11NOV01 we wish to confirm that we have frozen account of "Barako Trading Company" held with our Deira branch . This account was opened on 20MAR1995 and other details are as follows.

Name of the customer	Account No	Account Type / CCY	Balance
BARAKO TRADING COMPANY	025-094798-001 (Current Account / AED)		AED377,154-63
	025-094798-100 (Current Account / USD)		USD 88,868-39

We are fowarding by courier the related account opening documents of this account for your perusal and further instructions.

Yours sincerely,

for HSBC Bank Middle East

G M Sequeira
Regional Manager Operations

HSBC Bank Middle East
Middle East Management Office
PO Box 66, Dubai, United Arab Emirates
Tel: 971-4-3535000 Fax 971-4-3531005
Telex: 45424 HSBCD EM Telegrams: Bactria Dubai
Web: www.hsbc.com

*Incorporated in England by Royal Charter 1889
with limited liability*

بنك إتش إس بي سي الشرق الأوسط
مكتب الإدارة الشرق الأوسط
ص . ب . ٦٦ ، دبي ، الإمارات العربية المتحدة
هاتف : ٣٥٣٥٠٠٠-٤-٩٧١ فاكس ٣٥٣١٠٠٥-٤-٩٧١
تلكس : HSBCD EM ١٥٤٢٤ برقياً ، باكتريا دبي
Web: www.hsbc.com

تأسس في إنجلترا بموجب براءة ملكية عام ١٨٨٩
مسئولية محدودة

HSBC ⟨X⟩   URGENT

Mr Saeed Abdulla Al-Hamiz
Executive Director   Total : 1 page
Banking Supervisio . & Examination Department
Central Bank of the UAE
P O Box 854
Abu Dhabi

Date: 12 November 2001

Our reference : ME M BOP 010273

Dear Mr Saeed,

Re: CENTRAL BANK NOTICE NO. 2/351/01 DATED 07NOV01

Further to our fax message dated 11NOV01, sent under reference no. UAE COO 010102, we wish to advise that we have identified the following personal customer records that carry the address of " Post Box No. 3313", Dubai.

Name of the customer	Account No	Account Type - CCY
1) Ahmed Sheikh Ali Samantar	025-105727-001	Current Account – AED

Nationality   -   Somali
PP No.   -   A0394279
Address:-
Baraco Trading Company
P O Box. 3313, Dubai

2) Abdullahi Halane Shurie	025-225160-050	Statement Savings – AED

Nationality   -   Somali
PP No.   -   A0648357
Address:-
Al Manshiya Group
P O Box. 3313, Dubai

Please advise whether the funds available in the above accounts should be frozen immediately.

Yours sincerely,

for HSBC Bank Middle East

Steve Freeman
Chief Operating Officer

HSBC Bank Middle East
Middle East Management Office
PO Box 66, Dubai, United Arab Emirates
Tel: 971-4-3535000 Fax 971-4-3531005
Telex: 45424 HSBCD EM Telegrams: Bactria Dubai
Web: www.hsbc.com

Incorporated in England by Royal Charter 1867
with limited liabilities

بنك إتش إس بي سي الشرق الأوسط
مكتب الإدارة للشرق الأوسط
ص ب ٦٦ ، دبي، الإمارات العربية المتحدة
هاتف: ٣٥٣٥٠٠٠-٤-٩٧١ فاكس: ٣٥٣١٠٠٥-٤-٩٧١
تلكس : ٤٥٤٢٤ HSBCD EM برقيا : باكتريا دبي
Web: www.hsbc.com

تأسس في إنجلترا بموجب ميثاق ملكي عام ١٨٦٧
مسئولية محدودة

HSBC & MARK RICH CONNECTIONS

During the examination of HSBC Sharjah, I observed substantial incoming remittances from Glencore International – Switzerland, reportedly owned by Mark Rich. The branch officials could not forward any explanations for such transfers and later on classified the account as a suspicious one.

A detailed report on the account is given below in HSBC's own words:

Mark Rich had been a fugitive since 1983, when he fled to Switzerland just before he was indicted in the United States for allegedly evading more than $48 million in taxes, committing fraud and participating in illegal oil deals with Iran.

The outgoing President Clinton gave Rich a last minute pardon, which became a hot controversial topic of debate not only in America but also all around the world.

It is also reported that during the Abache regime, one of Nigeria's main trading partner was Glencore. Mark Rich currently denies any ownership of Glencore – he sold it long ago.

Mark Rich's association with Russians is well known to the world and a couple of other accounts like Baglan Trading at HSBC were regularly receiving large inward remittances from Glencore and the bank management simply kept their eyes closed.

MONEY LAUNDERING SUSPICIOUS REPORT

Customer	Azer Euro Trading LLC P O Box 20198 Ajman Account No. 040-256067-001
Nature of Business	Foodstuff Trading

Azer Euro Trading LLC(AET) a limited liability company has been operating in Ajman under a Trade Licence issued by Ajman Municipality since November 1999. The licence permits the company to Import/Export and Trade in foodstuff.

The Shareholders of AET are:-

1) Sh Salem Bin Mohd Al shamsi(SBM), UAE National (60%)
2) Hafiz Mammadev(HM), Azerbaijan National (40%)

SBM is also one of the directors of United Foods Company (Psc) Dubai, and HM is the General Manager/Partner of Alpha Plus, Azerbaijan, a grade '3' customer of HSBC Baku. By a Board Resolution HM is fully authorised to act on behalf of the company (typical expatriate ownership).

Our discussions with SBM and HM reveals that AET are also trading in Petroleum Products (Jet fuel, Petrol, Gasoline etc.) in large quantities, sourced from Azerbaijan/Georgia for Glencore International AG, Switzerland on a regular basis; under a contract signed between themselves, for onward delivery to third parties around the world.

The company has been receiving large Inward Remittances in USD since opening of this account in Sharjah in November 1999. All large wire transfers are received from Switzerland by order of Glencore International. We understand that these transactions are outside the purview of AETs business in UAE.

We have been allowing AET to continue operating their account mainly based on the recommendation of Mr Kamran Ulukhanov, Manager Corporate Banking, HSBC Baku. HM advises that regular Inward Remittances are expected from Glencore and are estimated to be around USD15.0M per annum.

Although we have no evidence of this customer being involved in any type of money laundering, we are unable to either understand fully the method of their dealings with Glencore or establish the credibility of Glencore AG. We have, however been sent by Mr Kamran a true copy of their agreement, which he has already sighted in Baku, but this appears to add minimal value.

In view of the above and involvement of our office in Baku , MEM OPS are hereby requested to advise us whether or not to continue this account relationship.

George Kappiuzhathu
Corporate Relationship Executive

BANKER TO MILLOSEVIC?

A reporter from the London Times had information about the existence of funds belonging to Millosevic, which were kept in the name of a Russian person. The newspaper sent a letter to that effect to the Governor and my opinion was sought. I had suggested that the answer should be sought from HSBC Management.

The Department wanted me to investigate, but for reasons better known to the Governor, no further action was taken and the file was closed. I can only say that with hundreds of Russian accounts opened and closed from time to time the possibility of the London Times' claim cannot be ruled out.

Later on in various staff meetings Sultan was heard criticizing HSBC, "How can I know that Millosevic related funds were parked here if the banks do not follow proper reporting to the Central Bank. Am I going to dream about the existence of such controversial accounts?"

THE SUNDAY TIMES

1 Pennington Street, London E1 9XW *Telephone: 020 7782 5000 Fax: 020 7782 5731*

تم استلامه بواسطة
دائرة الرقابة والتفتيش على المصارف

2 8 OCT 2000
الوقت :
التوقيع :

Thursday 26th October 2000

The Governor's Office,
Central Bank of the United Arab Emirates.

Your Excellency,

It is most kind of you to receive this fax and to give it your attention. I am a journalist on The Sunday Times and have worked here for one year. Before that I worked at the BBC. I would like to think that my reputation is as a fair-minded and honest journalist who works for the public good.

Recently, it has come to my attention that £44 million worth of money 'belonging' to Marko Milosevic, the son of the former Serbian ruler, passed through the UAE banking system in 1997. The money was deposited by a Russian man - whose identity we are not sure of but which is likely to be a man called Aslanov - into a numbered 'gold prima VIP account' at the British Bank of the Middle East in Dubai, what is now known as the Hong Kong and Shanghai Banking Corporation (HSBC).

These monies had come from an off-shore bank in Cyprus, believed to be the Karic Bank. In early 1999 the money was moved to HSBC Hong Kong branch and from there onwards to China, which may or may not have been its final destination.

Your Excellency, to my knowledge no law was broken at any time broken in these transactions. I understand that your senior counter money-laundering officials at the central bank were aware of who the money belonged to and kept track of its movement.

At the time, there was no imperative or, for that matter, justification for the UAE Central Bank which monitored the deposit of the £44 million to prevent any movement of the money.

Registered Office: Times Newspapers Limited, P.O. Box 495, Virginia Street, London E1 9XY Registered No. 894646 England

Letter from Sunday Times inquiring about Millosevic funds at HSBC Dubai

The FRY is now very keen to know the whereabouts of any such monies and to recover them. It is with this in mind that I ask you, with the utmost humbleness and respect, to inquire with your money-laundering officials as to the final destination of the £44 million as I am uninformed as to the name of the bank in China where the money was transferred to.

I have contacted HSBC in London. Their official statement has been: "We have not been able to find any evidence to support these allegations. HSBC has well established anti-money laundering policies and these are enforced rigorously throughout the Group and all the countries and territories where it operates. We have no further comment to make."

Your Excellency, I have great respect for your country and have a number of friends who have some power and influence in the UAE. It was through these 'friends' that I was able to come about the information I have set out to you.

In 1997 there was no reason to believe that Mr Milosevic was in any way linked to criminal activities. I have indicated to HSBC my willingness to see their actions in the best possible light of the changing politics of the Balkan countries. I have also made it clear that I am not in any way suggesting any illegal activities.

I understand that last November the UAE Central Bank indicated to the government that it would be keen to step up the fight against 'money-laundering'. It for this reason and because I know that as the head of your government's central bank your integrity is beyond question that I ask you to now make clear the finer details of these transactions which your officials monitored but could not prevent.

Your Excellency, HSBC has a reputation to protect, of course. But at the same time so does the UAE and its reputation is far vaster, older and more venerable than one bank. These matters are currently being pursued by a number of investigatory bodies worldwide. At what point will they become public? It is your power to protect HSBC from these questions or to protect the truth and the integrity of the UAE Central Bank's money-monitoring system in one swift stroke.

May I make one final point. Your officials in the money-laundering department at the central bank are of the highest standard both professionally and personally. Yet there is a common belief that they are blind to the activities of money-launderers and do not care, a belief reinforced by the public statements of treasury officials of the government of the United States of America.

Let us prove them wrong today.

Yours Sincerely,
Mr Adam George Nathan
Reporter: The Sunday Times
TEL: + 44 207 782 5688
FAX: +44 207 782 5542/5731

DEFRAUDING AN INSURANCE COMPANY ?

The top management of all the banks operating in the UAE is expatriate staff. Some of them indulge in underhanded dealings and bribes are solicited to approve loans. One such man was reported by me to Mohamed Sharif, who immediately contacted the Chief Executive of that bank and I understand following an inquiry his services were terminated later. An important UK bank's credit manager disbursed a substantial loan to an expatriate borrower without obtaining the required collaterals which were specified in the loan agreement. Later on the businessman fled from UAE leaving substantial debts to bankers, suppliers and other creditors. As soon as his disappearance was made public, the Credit Manager also ran away to Mumbai, on the next flight.

A similar case happened at one of HSBC's subsidiary.

All banks follow some basic lending norms like obtaining collaterals first and then, allowing the customer to draw on the loan. In this instance, it is hard to digest that the bank officials allowed the customer to withdraw funds and were left at the mercy of the customer to pass on the collateral later. When a bank lends against the collateral of shares, additional steps have to be taken to register the bank's interest on the share register of the company whose shares are pledged. None of these was implemented and some sort of collusion with the client cannot be ruled out.

Further, when the loan advanced to the customer is a substantial one like this, which was even higher than the bank's capital; bank officials are required to monitor such activity very closely.

HSBC, I am afraid, overlooked such basic procedures. The insurance company should once again review this claim and the shareholders should query the Board of Directors to justify this substantial questionable activity.

When the case was submitted to Sultan in due course it was brushed aside with the remark, "Don't fight other people's wars. The issue is between the Bank and Insurance Company and is not our problem," and tossed it aside.

Dear reader, read this episode in HSBC's own words and decide whether everything was fine at HSBC's UAE Branches, as claimed by the Management and on their accusation that I was simply taking revenge.

المُ

The Executive Director
Banking Supervision and Examination Department
Central Bank of UAE
P O Box 854
Abu Dhabi   27 November 2001

Our Ref: HFSM CEO 010821

Dear Sir

LOAN OF USD4M TO ALI REDHA DARWISH AL LAWATI

Further to our letter of 25 March 2001 rescheduling the above loan (Central Bank approval reference 10/390/2001 dated 28/3/2001), we are writing to advise the Central Bank that we have become aware of a probable fraud by the client in the provision of the security to cover the outstanding loan.

Background
Ali Redha Darwish Al Lawati, an Omani national, has been known to us for more than five years and a client of our sister company HSBC Bank Middle East for many years.

In January 2000, ARD as chairman of Majan International Bank ("Majan") was responsible for the acquisition by Commerzbank of a 15% interest in Majan. At this point he was Chairman of five public companies in Oman and a director of several others.

On 26 April 2000, HSBC Financial Services (Middle East) Limited ("HFSM"), lent the sum of US Dollars 4.75 million to ARCOM against certain securities following the approval from UAE Central Bank (approval reference 10.58.2000 dated 19/4/2000). The loan was initially granted for 90 days and then extended for a further six months (UAE Central Bank approval reference 10/140/2000 dated 30/7/2000). This was subsequently extended for a further 9 months (UAE Central Bank approval reference 10/390/2001 dated 28/3/2001). Total repayments totalling USD 1million were received. The key security was 1,950,000 shares in Majan International Bank ("MIB") SAOC. The security taken also comprised shares in National Sugar Refining Co. SAOG and Salalah Hilton SAOG. Additional security comprised post-dated cheques and a personal guarantee.

The approximate market value of the security at the time of granting the loan was USD 14 million of which the MIB shares were worth around USD 8 million. On 22nd May 2001, we took additional security of 100,000 Moller International Inc. and 518,000 Series B Preferred Stock of Cyberplus Corporation, together worth around USD 500,000.

HSBC Financial Services (Middle East) Limited
Investment Banking
PO Box 4604, Dubai, United Arab Emirates
Tel: 971-4-2288999 Fax: 971-4-2273301
Telex: 45806 WARDUB EM Telegrams: Bactria Dubai
Web: www.hsbc.com

Incorporated in Dubai by Royal Decree with limited liability

HSBC للخدمات المالية (الشرق الأوسط) المحدودة
الخدمات المصرفية الإستثمارية
ص ب : ٤٦٠٤ ، دبي ، الإمارات العربية المتحدة
هاتف : ٩٧١.٤.٢٢٨٨٩٩٩ فاكس : ٩٧١.٤.٢٢٧٣٣٠١
تلكس : ٤٥٨٠٦ WARDUB EM برقيا : باكتريا دبي
Web: www.hsbc.com

During a meeting in September 2001, the client advised that he had made a mistake and had been under the impression that we had taken over a London property and certain American securities instead of the MIB shares. The MIB shares, held by him for us, had been pledged elsewhere and had then been sold. He confirmed that he had nothing from us to justify his impression and that indeed our correspondence was absolutely clear as to what had been intended. Arising, from the fraudulent misuse of security, we have called an Event of Default under the Facility Agreement, such that all Indebtedness is now due.

Accordingly we have started implementing steps to make a claim under our insurance policy against fraud. We await formal confirmation from the insurance company of their verification of our claim. In view of the situation, we have prudently decided to make a provision in our books during November 2001 for the full amount of the loan whose outstanding amounted to AED14.26m as at 31OCT01. This will result in a shortfall of AED9.7m in our capital as at 31OCT01. In order to cover the shortfall in our regulatory minimum capital, our shareholders have agreed to provide a temporary shareholder loan of AED14.26m on the understanding that it will be repaid from future profits and any insurance refund that might be received subsequently in respect of the loan to Ali Redha. We are confident of receiving the insurance proceeds in respect of this claim during 2003.

Yours faithfully
for and on behalf of
HSBC Financial Services (Middle East) Limited

Mukhtar Hussain
Chief Executive Officer

THE ALGERIAN FISH

In the middle of 2002, the Central Bank of Algeria approached the UAE Central Bank to investigate certain documentary collections originating from Dubai to various buyers in Algeria. Under documentary collections, a seller or exporter approaches his bank and hands a set of shipping documents for onwards delivery to the buyer or importer. The bank in the seller's/exporter's country sends the shipping documents to the bank's correspondent in the country of the buyer/importer – Algeria in this case. The documents are handed over to the buyer/importer upon settling the payment, or agreeing to pay by accepting the Bill of Exchange accompanying the shipping documents.

An important document called a Bill of Lading (which serves as a proof that the goods have been shipped and is also a document to title) is an important part of the shipping documents. Apparently, no bill of lading was available and as such no goods were ever exported to Algeria. Further the shipping documents were handed back to the seller/exporter and not routed through the bank's correspondent in Algeria. The whole exercise was a sham and the series of transactions was made to look like a real export-import procedure solely to draw out substantial funds from Algeria to Dubai.

The funds in Dubai were immediately withdrawn or wired out. All the sellers/exporters operating out of Dubai had closed their shops and were untraceable.

One does not have to be an expert banker to detect such schemes, and during my examination of HSBC, I had picked up various transactions and had pointed them out to Sultan. Even HSBC's internal auditor was concerned that the bank was being used as a conduit for money laundering. An excerpt from their Audit Report of Sharjah Branch for May 2000 is given below. The Financial Action Task Force, which attempts to control the dirty funds in the international world, should approach both the Algerian and UAE Central Banks to forward details of each and every transaction for review. I will not be surprised if later on the authorities conclude that they were terror-related finances.

All the transactions were in US dollars and were routed through US correspondent banks, thereby abusing the US Banking System. The US bank regulators should review these transactions.

I would love to organize a technical workshop for John Bond & company. They badly need some lessons on how to run a bank in an ethical manner.

I always have a hearty laugh when various organizations confer super titles and awards to HSBC even calling it the best bank in the world. They will slap themselves after reading my book.

GROUP AUDIT MIDDLE EAST   GAM GEN 000010

GENERAL AUDIT OF HBME SHARJAH   MAY 2000

5.2   **Exports**

5.2.1   Collection Documents

Finding

The auditors were unable to satisfy themselves that OBCs handled on behalf of one client (040-105298-001) covering exports to Algeria were for legitimate purposes.

- Bills of lading were not obtained from a reputed shipper but from a freight forwarder which was not listed on the pre-approved shipping list.
- All invoices were addressed to individuals in Algeria.
- Although collection orders had been prepared these were not mailed directly to the Algerian Bank (collecting bank) but instead handed back to the customer along with the original invoices.
- Trade terms were 90-120 days. However, bills were generally settled within 30 -35 days.
- The majority of funds received had been withdrawn in cash (AED7 million in MAR/APR00).

Risk

The Bank being used as a conduit for money laundering.

Recommendation

Steps should be taken to identify the precise nature of this company's business transactions with Algeria in an attempt to confirm their legitimacy. Furthermore, collection orders should not be accepted from the customer, in future, unless all relevant shipping documents are forwarded directly by HBME to a correspondent bank in Algeria for collection.

Excerpt from Internal Audit Report on HSBC Sharjah Branch – Algerian issue.

THE BIG APPLE BITES

They say New York is a land of opportunities and I did come across one bank account involving substantial funds moving from New York to Dubai. The lucky person in this case was working for an airline and drawing a small salary but suddenly receives millions and millions of dollars from New York, which was claimed by him as profits from investing on the stock exchange in the USA.

The HSBC management must have realized that this was a white lie because the salary, which he was earning in Dubai, would barely meet his basic needs without leaving any funds for investment. The compliance officer wrote to Bagley for his guidance – Bagley directed the incoming funds should be sent back to New York and concluded that such cases should not be "tipped" to the Central Bank.

In my opinion, HSBC should have informed the UAE Central Bank and sought guidance. The possibility that the funds were tainted cannot be ruled out.

The Compliance officers report is given below:

SCHEDULE 2

Ref No

HSBC GROUP   Form compiled Sept.'93

MONEY LAUNDERING SUSPICION REPORT

Please complete this form in as much detail as possible and return it to your relevant MLCO:

SOURCE

Group Entity	HSBC Bank Middle East		
Office Address	Deira Branch, Nasr Square, Deira, Dubai, UAE		
Your Name	Mohd A Amiri		
Your Reference		Tel. No.	04-2074225
Your Signature		Fax No.	04-249490
Date of Report	19JUN99		

SUSPICION

Name of Account Holder	Amir Ali		
Account No.	025-336199-211		Date of Birth :
Occupation			
Address			

DETAILS OF SUSPICION :

Please provide details of suspicious transactions and other relevant data. Attach a separate sheet if necessary. (Include other suspects, nationality, etc. Attach copy Ids, transaction notes).

Mr. Amir Ali is a staff of Air Lanka drawing a salary of around AED8,000/- which is credited to his Current Account. The customer received three large inward remittances from Bank of New York, New York i.e. USD1,439,808.10 & USD1,043,502.85 & USD200,000/-. We interviewed the customer and he advised us that the transfers were made by his cousin who is a US Residentand the funds were sale proceeds of equity in which they had invested jointly. The account holder willingly agreed to return the funds when we advised him that we were not comfortable in handling such large funds for him.

Other territories involved in the transaction :

12/97   19/19   Complaince Officer Handbook

Suspicious Activity Report not filed with the Central Bank and picked up by me during the examination.

MASTER STROKE BY HSBC GROUP MANAGEMENT

In the English cricket team, after the departure of Ian Botham there was a big vacuum, which now has been adequately filled by the arrival of Andrew Flintoff. Both the cricketers in their day had the ability to take the game away from their opponent by their powerful stroke play. I think HSBC is also not far away.

During the course of our raid on HSBC Branches, there was a sudden and simultaneous transfer of key senior management and a new team took over the helm of their UAE management in July 2000. No sensible management will transfer so many top executives at the same time from a region but this was a master stroke by the HSBC Group management. It hindered our examination, because the successor was ignorant of the issues. The executives moved were then out of the reach of the UAE judicial system. The old gang knew too much about the questionable deeds, so they were moved out.

Most of them were promoted, with Coverdale and Dawe striking super-jackpots – promoted as Executive

Director and Deputy Head of Malaysian and Indian operations, respectively. The executives transferred were:

John Coverdale – Chief Operating Officer
Phillips Dawe -Manager Internal Audit Gulf Region
Alistar Currie – Manager HSBC Jebel Ali Branch
Keith O'Connors –Manager Call Centre
David Proud – Senior Manager Personal Banking
Jeff Eggleton – Senior Manager Abu Dhabi Branch
Robbin Barnes- Managing Director HSBC MEFCO

It was also observed that spouses of two executives were in employment at HSBC at senior levels. This completely violates the general banking norms, and close relatives are never employed. The concerned spouses were:

Su Barnes- Manager Credit
Joy O'Connors – Manager Training

On investigations with the Head of the Personnel Department, we were told overall more than fifty employees have close relatives employed at various positions at HSBC Middle East.

I had repeatedly requested a list of close relatives employed by the Bank, and this was promised, but it seems promises at HSBC were meant to be broken and the list never arrived. It would be interesting to review this list.

HSBC was taking a dangerous risk because two authorized signatories can bring a bank down by their fraudulent acts. Another basic control, which was overlooked by the Management, was rotation of key personnel from time to time and the Senior Branch Manager of their Deira Branch was not rotated for more than a decade from his post.

Later on, David Bagley, who should have been behind bars in the UAE, was also promoted handsomely from being the Compliance Head for Gulf Operations to Head of Group Compliance in the UK.

John Bond who is an expert on giving lecturers on integrity, honesty, ethics and accountability should take a tip from Citibank, which fired key senior staff on accountability issues in October, 2004, following recent problems in Japan where regulators ordered the closure of Citigroup's private bank. Let me see what drastic action he will take following the publication of my book against the erring staff of HSBC Bank.

The English batsmen do not believe in "walking" when they are out and the Umpires supervising the cricket matches have to give them marching orders. I am sure Bond will also not "walk". Just as cricket is no longer a gentlemen's game with match fixing and drug scandals, banking too is no longer a gentlemanly profession and regulators are required to regulate their activities. When John Bond started his banking career there were no regulators and now even 370 world wide regulators of HSBC Group do not have the courage to use the whip.

PINCHING FUNDS FROM CUSTOMERS' ACCOUNTS

I am told that in the UK, which happens to be the home of HSBC, the most popular crime committed by men is "'bottom pinching" and a friend had told a joke on this subject. As the joke goes – The husband and his wife were in the elevator and in came a stunning butterfly wearing an ultra modern dress. The husband was intoxicated by her arrival, but had to control his naughty desire. After some time, the pretty girl slaps the husband on his cheek and walks away. The poor husband is seen swearing to his wife that he was innocent and the wife coolly says, "Darling don't swear. I know you did not pinch her, because for a change, I pinched her."

Well at HSBC Middle East, both the male and female staff love to pinch money from customers' bank accounts. Saeed Jabri was also involved in defrauding customers in many ways, stealing money and also borrowing from them.

My favorite Bollywood writer, Kadar Khan, who is known for his enterprising dialogue, will give me 10 points on a scale of 10 for defining HSBC as follows in my Indian Hindi language:

H – Hum
S – Subse
B – Bade
C – Chor Hai

Meaning: we are the biggest thieves.

Read these two cases and you will concur with my definition.

To   Distribution   02Feb1999
From   COVERDALE J E BBME MEM   COO   Tel 971 4 5077681
Our Ref MEM COO 990019   Your Ref
Subject FRAUD

In a recent fraud experienced at one of our branches a third party
presented a letter of authority(ostensibly issued by a savings
account holder) authorising the payment of cash to the bearer of the
letter.

The cash was paid after verifying the letter (which was forged).When
the customer disputed the transaction the branch realised that the
voucher (and the attached customer's letter)were missing from the
voucher bundle.

The above case revealed a number of control lapses and these are
articulated below for the benefit of all Areas:

1.   A large sum of cash was paid to a third party even though the
     Savings statement/passbook rules preclude such payments under
     any circumstances.

2.   The teller supervisor initialled the teller total cards
     without physically counting the cash.

3.   The executive did not arrange for the counting of vouchers at
     the end of the day either in his presence or in that of the
     Input Output Officer.

4.   The executive allowed staff to retrieve vouchers the next day
     without personal supervision.

5.   The security camera was only activated when the remote alarm
     was triggered. The transaction was therefore not captured by
     the camera.

The fraud emphasises the importance of the controls required over
vouchers and in this respect attention is drawn to BIM VOL 2 Sec
91.9, General HUB Procedure Manual Sec 16 and the NFC ADM manual (for
the UAE) SEC MAD OPS 110.

Please be guided accordingly.

Yours sincerely,

J.E.Coverdale
Chief Operating Officer, UAE
[Sent by MAGGIE(LOCAL)]

Dist   INGLIS R T   BBME BAF   CEO
         JONES G V   BBME LBM   DCE
         BRAY R J   BBME JOM   CEO

A staff related fraud case not reported to the Central Bank
but picked up during the examination – Shows the level of
staff integrity and honesty.

Abdul Rahim Sinkais, heads the Anti-money Laundering & Suspicious Case Unit at the UAE Central Bank. In my opinion, Sinkas is a very dedicated and honest person and has a soft spot for me. Earlier, Sinkais was one of the UAE liquidators of BCCI, and I had the opportunity to work for two months as the Acting Secretary to the Liquidators.

Salim Mushtaq, who was the permanent Secretary, had recommended me to run the show in his absence. Sinkais was closely following our HSBC investigations and was very impressed with the progress, and it so happened that a sensational Congo Promissory Note Fraud case at a leading foreign Bank came up and Sinkais asked Nasr and me to investigate this one also. So in the morning we were covering the Congo case in Dubai and in the afternoon we were at HSBC Sharjah.

One day we were driving from Dubai to Sharjah when my mobile phone rang. Nasr was driving but his ears were glued to the conversation I was having with a dear friend working for Abu Dhabi Capital Radio station.

My friend informed me that his colleague's ex- wife was arrested by the Sharjah Police on a complaint filed by her employers. The wife was attached to the HSBC Credit Card Unit, which was operating from the first floor of HSBC Sharjah. His colleague also spoke to me and requested my assistance.

I could hardly believe my luck that we could get such a tip out of the blue, when we were investigating their Sharjah Branch. We were also surprised that the HSBC Management failed to inform us about this extraordinary credit card fraud. The next day Nasr and myself went to meet the Manager of their Credit Card unit which actually caters to their entire Gulf region.

I asked the Manager if everything was normal and the reply was in the affirmative. I inquired the whereabouts of that female staff member, and then he confessed that she was in the custody of the Sharjah Police. As soon as he completed that sentence, Nasr got angry and asked him why he lied by telling us that everything is fine at their card unit. We were then briefed about the modus operandi, which involved a couple of bank staff and some outsiders.

The fraud came to light when one of their credit card holders complained that her card was used to draw out cash from the various ATM's in UAE, but during that period she vacationing abroad.

KPMG – THE BLIND
GLOBAL AUDITORS
OF HSBC

My great grandparents were practicing HAKIMS, traditional doctors by profession, but I am not a practicing HAKIM and as such cannot certify medically whether KPMG are totally blind, half blind, partially blind, color blind or night blind.

As an auditor I can say that KPMG being the global auditors are the only people who had complete access to the worldwide operations of HSBC. All I know that at HSBC Middle East, the Branch compliance officers, the internal audit reports and the Regional Compliance Head - all of them had knowledge that they were involved in ML (money laundering) activities. If regulators like me can read their memos and reports, I don't know why KPMG auditors could not read the writing on the wall.

They were also aware that twenty auditors from the Central Bank had raided their client and had summoned FSA from the UK. Certainly something must be wrong some where?

I do not know whether the incriminating records were hidden from KPMG auditors and if that was not the case, then certainly their auditing techniques and standards are extremely poor and should certainly take steps to correct them.

The billion-dollar question that comes to mind is whether KPMG compromised and turned a blind eye by issuing an unqualified report for HSBC Middle East Bank. I am afraid I can't answer this one. It would be an interesting scenario, if a shareholder takes them to court accusing them of gross negligence in performing their duties, and then perhaps one would know something from the horse's mouth. Otherwise they will remain silent forever.

I have passed them a copy of a letter written to the Board of HSBC Group, seeking the resignation of their Group chairman Sir John Bond, who at that time was also the Chairman of HSBC Middle East, along with the written evidence of my allegations. KPMG's New York office has confirmed the receipt of my communication and has indicated that the matter is being investigated at the appropriate level.

There are now two legal implications, which are summarized below:

1.) When an auditor becomes aware of information concerning a possible illegal act, SAS no. 54 requires him or her to obtain from senior management information on the act's nature, the circumstances under which it occurred and its possible effect on the client's financial statements.

If the management does not provide conclusive evidence that an illegal act has not occurred, the standard requires the auditor to consult with the client's legal counsel or other specialists about how relevant laws apply to the situation and the impact it may have on the financial statements.

In cases where the auditor concludes the act is illegal and could have a material effect on the entity's financial statements, he or she must inform its management and the audit committee of it immediately.

2.) Under Section 10A of the Securities Exchange Act of 1934, if the management does not take "timely and appropriate remedial action" to address the illegal act, the auditor must report the situation to the board of directors. If the auditor does not receive confirmation that the board reported the act to the SEC within one day of receiving notice of it, the auditor must either resign or, by the following day, give the SEC a copy of his or her report to the board.

HSBC's shares are listed on the NY Exchange, hence the UK banking giant now falls under the jurisdiction of the US Securities Exchange Commission and it would be interesting to see the future step KPMG takes. As the global auditors of the HSBC group they have simply shut their eyes for certain events in which their client is involved. They are required to open their eyes.

The latest CIA report claims that Saddam Hussein has used the HSBC branch in Jordan to avoid UN Trade Sanctions. US investigation of Riggs Bank showed ten wire transfers were sent from the controversial E G oil bank account to Apexside Trading, aggregating to $ 8.1 million, banking with HSBC in Luxembourg and Cyprus. The HSBC management in the US agreed to such transfer but did not reveal the names of the owners/beneficiaries using the veil of confidentiality at Luxembourg and Cyprus Operations.

In 2002 the Spanish authorities came down heavily on HSBC for some 138 accounts opened for wealthy businessmen containing around Sterling 40 million. HSBC transferred two executives from their Madrid operations. Again in 2002, the Argentine police raided several foreign banks. HSBC was one of them, pursuant to a court investigation into large scale illegal capital flight in the range of $30 billion from Argentina.

Reports indicate that the UK authorities were aware of some USD $6 million moved to HSBC Group for General Abacha related bank accounts.

The US banking regulators in 2003 had compelled HSBC USA Bank to enter into an agreement to tighten anti-money laundering procedures and practices. Despite the pressure from everywhere, HSBC knows the art of keeping the wolf away. However KPMG, as global auditors, have access to every HSBC unit in the world and let's wait for their decision.

All these years, they have been giving unqualified reports of clean health regarding HSBC's operations... are they going to divert from their earlier ways?

LEGAL PENALTIES FOR MONEY LAUNDERING

David Bagley had written to his bosses in London that in the absence of any money laundering laws in the UAE no local regulations have been broken and no report on money laundering will be made to the UAE Central Bank. He also indicated to me in a separate letter that no report has yet been made to any Regulators of HSBC. According to John Bond, their Group Chairman, HSBC has some 370 regulators worldwide.

As most of the funding was routed through the US, the bank certainly has misused the US banking system and its own internal regulations on money laundering have been breached. They have showed scant respect for the UK regulations despite being a UK based entity. HSBC agreed that their Sharjah Branch was involved in laundering funds for Victor Bout-related accounts (extracts from their internal audit report are given below), but our investigation revealed that this was only the tip of the iceberg.

As per current US laws, a financial institution can be subject to the following penalties for money laundering:

Federal Criminal Conviction for money laundering:

- A prison term up to 20 years
- Fine of up to $ 500,000 or twice the value of funds laundered

Conviction for violating record keeping and reporting requirements:
- Fines and penalties
- Up to 10 years for willful violations

A criminal conviction for money laundering requires proof of an individual's knowing, or willful participation in transactions designed to conceal the source or nature of criminal proceeds or to avoid reporting requirements. Further a criminal conviction can be based on an individual's willful blindness to circumstances that would alert a reasonable person that a transaction was designed to launder money or conscious avoidance of information that would plainly expose the illicit nature of transactions. Similarly an individual who has engaged in willful blindness is equally as guilty as an active participant in the scheme. HSBC officials were fully aware of the issues and I don't see what defense they can offer legally.

In the UK, criminal offense for money laundering covers a potential sentence up to 14 years. The UK laws are quite stringent, and in addition to reporting domestic money laundering (ML) transactions to the National Criminal Intelligence Service (NCIS), the financial institutions are obliged to report overseas offenses to NCIS. The offense of failing to report to NCIS that an individual is engaged in ML applies to all aspects of ML including ML abroad that would amount to an offense if it took place in the UK.

Failure to disclose may also give grounds to be charged with the offense of ML itself, which carries a maximum penalty of 14 years imprisonment in the UK. In view of the legal provisions, HSBC was statutorily required to report ML activities at their UAE operations to NCIS. I don't know whether HSBC has complied with the UK laws. The Financial Service Authority, which had heavily fined Abbey National with a record fine of STG 2.32 million, Bank of Ireland for STG 375,000 and Bank of Scotland for STG 1.25 million for breaches of ML rules and compliance failures have confirmed to me that they are investigating my complaint against HSBC.

The US Authorities are sleeping over the case for more than 1.5 years despite being aware that dirty funds in millions and millions of dollars from Russia/CIS passed though HSBC NY into the UAE while countless others were penalized for similar issues. Some months back I had approached Federal Reserve Bank of NY which had compelled HSBC USA to sign an agreement to tighten up their anti-money laundering operations.

One of their senior lawyers, Martin Grant, replied to my email confirming that they know me very well because US Homeland Security Officials had visited FED with my reports. When I inquired what actions FED had taken as my life was in danger, the FED officials started avoiding me.

In 1991 the US Regulators imposed a record fine of $200 million on BCCI, (majority owned by Abu Dhabi) which admitted money laundering and recently $25 million on Riggs Bank and other banks have also been fined on account of breaches in its anti-money laundering controls, but HSBC gets away everywhere.

In the UAE, the law of the jungle prevails –"Might makes right" HSBC got away using its power, despite my complaints to various UAE authorities. On the lighter side, they must have realized that scores are settled because the Middle East judiciary is run on the principle "an eye for an eye and a tooth for a tooth"- Our banks were involved in doing something in the UK, so if their bank is involved in something here, then the case is closed – justice has been served.

The philosophy of the UAE law can be summed up in this case: A British director along with his troupe came to perform in Abu Dhabi and a new butterfly, who is now a popular artiste, headed straight for a beach, took off her clothes and dived naked to cool herself. The police arrested the Director and held him accountable for the action of this beautiful sexy starlet.

Complaints were lodged with the UN and Financial Action Task Force, but HSBC officers (who agreed being launderers but will not inform the regulators) and Suweidi continue to live happily while the auditor who exposes their misdeeds continues to receive threats to his life.

" By hook or by crook, we will get you from India." I understand a RED ARREST WARRANT has been placed with Indian Authorities to arrest me when I land in India. A well-wisher of mine has recently indicated to me that the UAE Courts have passed a judgment in absentia sentencing me to death.

(ii)   **Andrii Semenchenko (ASM)** maintains an active personal AIG account
        at SHJ and also either operates or is connected with a number of other
        accounts on which substantial activity, some of a potentially dubious
        nature, has taken place (see appendix 3 for details). These accounts
        include:-

a)   San Air General Trading FZE WLL ("San Air") which is a
        sole proprietorship of ASM, registered in the Ajman Free Zone.
        San Air's account had been personally introduced to SHJ in
        JUL98 by SAJ. Although registered in Ajman, the Company
        has a Dubai postal address. A number of unusual transactions
        (including large cash transactions and transfers to a local money
        exchange) have taken place over this account over the past year
        (as summarised in appendix 3).

b)   Mardiboy Kakharov (MK) is an Uzbeki national and is
        believed to be closely connected with San Air. MK has
        provided ASM with a Power of Attorney to operate his personal
        account on his behalf. The account opening form showed that
        MK earned a monthly salary of AED3,000. However, credit
        turnover, aggregating AED5.6 million between DEC98 and
        FEB99, is clearly not commensurate with this level of salary.
        The credit turnover included one inward remittance for
        AED2.38 million emanating from the Uzbekistan Ministry of
        Defence, the proceeds of which were disbursed to various
        parties, including ASM controlled accounts.

c)   GMS General Trading WLL ("GMS") is another sole
        proprietorship registered in the Ajman Free Zone, owned by
        Olena Semenchenko (believed to be ASM's wife). The GMS
        account had been introduced by San Air in DEC98. ASM had
        originally been given a Power of Attorney to operate this
        account. In APR99, this Power of Attorney was replaced by a
        Power of Attorney in favour of MK. Activity over this account
        includes a large round-robin transaction for AED2 million
        involving MK's and San Air's respective accounts.

GAM's Observations

i)   Based on our review, we are not comfortable with SHJ's dealings with the
        Semenchenko "Group" or with the unknown extent and nature of SAJ's
        involvement with and/or borrowings from ASM. Specifically, we are of the
        opinion that the nature and size of some of the transactions should have been
        queried by SHJ OPS Manager (who was responsible for reviewing the
        exception reports) and should also have been brought to the attention of the
        UAE MLCO.

Appendix 3

Major Account Activity over Semenchenko
Related Accounts

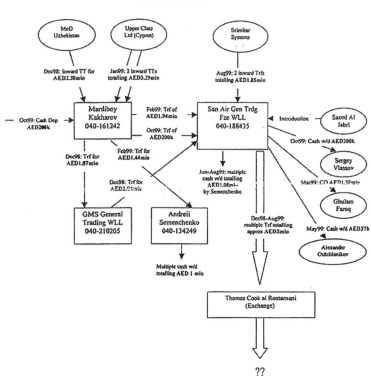

??

Extracts from HSBC Sharjah Branch's Internal Audit
Report on Victor Bout-related bank accounts including San
Air.

PAUL O'NEIL VISITS UAE

The papers were buzz with O'Neil, the US Treasury Secretary's fact-finding mission to the UAE. The grapevine in the financial circle about his visit centered around two missions: one to determine whether treasury gold stock from the Taliban Government made way into the Dubai Gold Market, and the other one was to meet Hawala operators to obtain first hand information on the Hawala System (the unofficial remittance system).

I understand O'Neil did visit the Gold Souk (Market) which is among the largest in the world with tons and tons of gold stocked with the wholesalers and countless retailers at all times.

The Souk is open up to midnight and during the holy month of Ramzan is open all night. Despite such huge stock of gold I have not heard about any big organized robbery although occasionally some small scale ones are heard from time to time but I will not be surprised if the Souk becomes a victim of a big one.

The views of Afghanistan gold in Dubai Souk was based on the fact that UAE was one of the few countries which had recognized the Taliban Government and their national airline was only flying to Dubai and back. Further tons and tons of the Treasuries gold could easily be sold in the billion-dollar Dubai Gold Market in a split second and funds moved to any part of the world in minutes through Hawala System of remittance.

I don't know if O'Neil was successful or not in tracing the Afghan gold to the Dubai Souk but what I know is that O'Neil could not meet any Hawala dealer. After all post 9/11 events, no Hawala dealers would risk exposing himself by meeting the US Treasury Secretary and walk him through a typical real Hawala transaction.

The third well guarded mission, which only a handful knew (not even me at that point of time) was his flying visit to the UAE Exchange Centre's Bur Dubai Branch, which is exactly opposite HSBC's Head Office and behind UAE Central Bank's Dubai Branch. O'Neil was escorted around sunset by none other than Mohammed Al Abbar, who at such a young age practically runs Dubai's financial sector. Al Abbar incidentally is an ex-UAE Central Bank official and very close to the Ruling Family of Dubai. Obaid Salami and myself were representing the UAE Central Bank.

Some months later during the course of my audit of UAE Exchange Centre, I picked up that the said exchange's bank account in New York was seized by FBI pertaining to funds transferred to Marwan Al Shhehi in Florida. According to the U.S. authorities, Marwan was one of the terrorists involved in 9/11 attacks on America.

On hindsight I realize that the usually jovial managing partner of UAE Exchange B R Shetty, a business baron and his Man Friday Sudhir Shetty were both rather nervous on the day of O'Neil's visit to their exchange. Shetty is now one of the richest Indians to hit the Gold Pot in UAE, having come here some thirty years back with less than ten dollars in his pocket and now having a net worth running into billions.

O'Neil asked some questions but at no time gave us the impression or even hints about the seizure. In the evening a dinner was organized for O'Neil and his delegation and while leaving the exchange, I waved to B R Shetty and said – See you at the dinner and he replied – I am not invited.

I was pretty surprised that Shetty was not invited at the dinner at which the cream of UAE's business magnets and galaxy of VIP's were assembled. I perhaps thought that there was some error or oversight at the Central Bank in not sending an invitation to him.

I quickly replied, "Come over as my guest."

Shetty attended the dinner party but neither the Governor nor the Deputy Governor or the Executive Director even glanced at him. Shetty soon realized that he was not welcome at that party.

In UAE circles, Shetty is an icon and hence could not digest the humiliation of being ignored by the hosts. He came over to me and said –" It seems your Governor does not like my presence and as I am not invited I am thinking of leaving". I told him that the Governor was very busy with the Treasury Secretary and he was not an uninvited guest because I had invited him. Hearing my support for him, Shetty did stay on for some time but I remember distinctly that after some time he was nowhere to be seen at the party.

Looking back, I now realize why Shetty was not invited to that dinner by the Governor, who was fully aware about the seizure of UAE exchange's bank account in New York and hence did not want Shetty anywhere near O'Neil. Shetty, on the other hand was fully aware why the Governor was neglecting him. Only I was ignorant of the mystery.

Iqbal Hakim, making a presentation to Mr Paul O Neil the then US Treasury Secretary who insisted in visiting the Bur Dubai Branch of UAE Exchange Centre, which transferred funds to a 9/11 terrorist. In the background is Mohammed Al Abbar (in Arabic Dress) B R Shetty the managing partner of the Exchange, has raised his "finger up". Shetty like me is a big cricket lover and the umpires in a cricket match, raise their finger to declare a batsman out. – Is he declaring himself out?

Certainly not, but in this instance two batsmen were given out - O Neil and me and currently both of us are living a life in wilderness. In US this raised finger means something else and in India it means I will take care of you - I understand a Supari (contract to kill) has been signed to eliminate me. I remember my mother's saying – Son, do not point a finger on somebody else because the remaining fingers actually points towards you.

Some other photos of the Treasury Secretary's historical visit to the UAE Exchange Centre following the 9/11 attack.

UAE EXCHANGE CENTRE AND THE 9/11 FINANCING

The 9/11 Commission Report says it is still not known where the money to fund the attack originated. The Report however estimates that the 9/11 operation cost between $400K - $500K. I entirely agree that it is extremely difficult to find the sources overseas, which would involve piercing through the secrecy laws that shelter many bank accounts. Further the US receives trillion of dollars in inward remittances and finding few thousand terrorist funds is again a difficult proposition. However a part of that sum was wired in from UAE Exchange Centre to a 9/11 terrorist in the USA.

Two former Central Bank employees using their spouse as fronts originally formed the UAE Exchange Centre some thirty years back or so. They misused their authority and got the name approved which in some sense gives a misleading impression to the world at large, that the exchange is owned by the State or has some sort of State support or patronage.

I don't know when and how B R Shetty became associated with this exchange, but heard that he took over from the former owners. However recently while searching on the net, I have picked up that one Mr. George claims to be the real partner of this exchange and that he was framed in a fabricated case and currently imprisoned in a mysterious Abu Dhabi jail. On the website www. UAEPrison.com one can read his story and his plight in the Al Wathba Prison, which it seems, is more notorious than the famous Abu Ghraib prison of Saddam Hussein. Human Rights activists from all over the world should turn their eyes on this one now and come to the rescue of countless inmates, who as the website says are living a life of hell.

Abdul Wahab, was my audit partner during the examination of the UAE Exchange and it was detected during the examination that in November 2001, the United States District Court Southern District of New York issued a seizure warrant on Citibank New York, commanding and authorizing the attachment of US$ 109,500 in the account of UAE Exchange Center A/c No 36215468. The seizure was made pursuant to an affidavit made by an FBI Agent, representing funds transferred to Marwan Al Shehhi's bank account in Florida through UAE Exchange Center Bur Dubai Branch. According to US authorities, Al Shehhia, is a prime suspect in the 9/11 terrorist attack on America. The details of the transfers made to Al Shehhia's are as follows:

Date Remitter Amount in $
July 18, 2000 Isam Mansur 10,000
August 5, 2000 Isam Mansur 9,500
August 29,2000 Ali 20,000
September 19,2000 Hani 70,000
Total US$ 109,500

The relevant documents explaining the seizure are given below:

11/23/01 FRI 12:25 FAX 212 657 3361   ....CITIBK CEEMEA...   ☒001

UNITED STATES DISTRICT COURT
SOUTHERN DISTRICT OF NEW YORK
- -

Post-it® Fax Note	7671	Date 11/23/01	# of pages ► 2
To Mr. RICHARD VACAN		From MURTAZA Firoß	
Co./Dept UAE Exchange		Co. CITIBANK NEW YORK	
Phone #		Phone # (212)657-5030	
Fax # (971?) 621-1447		Fax # (212) 657-1156	

UNITED STATES OF AMERICA   :

            -v-   :   Mag. Dkt. No. 01-

$109,500 IN ACCOUNT NO.   :
36215468 IN THE NAME OF
UAE EXCHANGE CENTRE L.L.C.   :
AT CITIBANK N.A.,
                                      :
          Defendant-in-rem.
                                      :
- - - - - - - - - - - - - - - - - -x

            SEIZURE WARRANT
       PURSUANT TO 18 U.S.C. § 981(b)

TO: ANY DESIGNATED SPECIAL AGENT OF THE FEDERAL BUREAU OF
      INVESTIGATION AND/OR ANY FEDERAL LAW ENFORCEMENT OFFICER
      AUTHORIZED BY LAW

      Affidavit having been made before me by Supervisory Special

Agent Daniel Gill, of the Federal Bureau of Investigation

("FBI"), that he has reason to believe that the above-captioned

funds are subject to seizure and civil forfeiture pursuant to 18

U.S.C. §§ 981(a)(1)(A), 981(a)(1)(C), 984 and 981(b), and as I am

satisfied that there is probable cause to believe that the

property so described is subject to seizure and civil forfeiture

pursuant to 18 U.S.C. §§ 981(a)(1)(A), 981(a)(1)(C), 984 and

981(b);

      · YOU ARE HEREBY COMMANDED AND AUTHORIZED to seize, within 10

days, by personally serving a copy of this warrant of seizure

upon appropriate officers of Citibank N.A., during regular

business hours, the following property: $109,500 IN ACCOUNT NO.

36215468 IN THE NAME OF UAE EXCHANGE CENTRE L.L.C. AT CITIBANK

N.A.

US Court seizure order seizing the Bank account of
UAE Exchange Centre for US$109,500 pertaining to funds
transferred to a 9/11 terrorist in the US

If said property is found to be present, leave a copy of
this warrant and receipt for this property seized or handed over
and return this warrant to this Court within 10 days as required
by law.

Dated: New York, New York
         November   , 2001

         NOV 2 0 2001

                                    _____
                                    UNITED STATES MAGISTRATE JUDGE
                                    SOUTHERN DISTRICT OF NEW YORK
                                         HENRY PITMAN
                                    United States Magistrate Judge
                                    Southern District of New York

U.S. Department of Justice

Federal Bureau of Investigation

Washington, D.C. 20535

January 18, 2002

Registered, Return Receipt

UAE Exchange Centre LLC
ATTN: Sudhir Kumar Shetty
P.O. Box 170
ABU DHABI, United Arab Emirates

Dear Sudhir Kumar Shetty:

Factual and Legal Basis for Seizure

On November 20, 2001, property was seized by the Federal Bureau of Investigation (FBI) at New York, New York for forfeiture for violation of MONEY LAUNDERING CONTROL ACT OF 1986. The property was appraised at $75,093.26 and is described as follows:

$75,093.26 from Account Number #36215468 in the name of UAE Exchange Centre at Citibank. (See Attached List)

Account Number: 36215468
Account Name: UAE Exchange Centre LLC
Financial Inst: Citibank
Asset Id Number: 02-FBI-000303
Seizure Number: 3540020033

The forfeiture is being conducted pursuant to Title 18, United States Code (U.S.C.), Section 981 and the following additional federal laws: 19 U.S.C. Sections 1602-1619 and 18 U.S.C. Section 983.

You may contest the seizure and forfeiture of this property and/or petition to the FBI and request a pardon of the forfeited property.

To Contest the Forfeiture

if you want to contest the seizure or forfeiture of the property in court, you must file a claim of ownership with the FBI by March 4, 2002. The claim is filed when it is received by the FBI Forfeiture Paralegal Specialist of the FBI Field Division mentioned below except in cases of pro se incarcerated individuals as otherwise provided by law. The claim need not be made in any particular form. The claim shall identify the specific property being claimed and state the claimant's interest in such property. Documentary evidence supporting claimant's interest in the property may help substantiate the claim, but is not required. The claim must be made under oath, subject to penalty of perjury. A frivolous claim may subject the claimant to a civil fine equal to ten (10) percent of the value of the forfeited property but in no event shall the fine be less than $250 or greater than $5,000.

To Request Release of the Property

Upon the filing of a claim a claimant, pursuant to 18 U.S.C. 983 (f), may request release of the seized property during pendency of forfeiture proceedings due to hardship. Property not subject to release under this provision includes: contraband, currency, or other monetary instrument, or electronic funds unless such currency or other monetary instrument or electronic funds constitutes the assets of a legitimate business; property to be used as evidence of a violation of law; property by reason of design or other characteristic is particularly suited for use in illegal activities; or property likely to be used to commit additional criminal acts if returned

FBI seizure documents seizing the funds of UAE Exchange Centre.

Sudhir Kumar Shetty

to the claimant.

To Request a Pardon of the Property

In addition to or in lieu of filing a claim, if you want to request a pardon of the forfeited property, submit a petition for remission or mitigation of the forfeiture to the FBI Field Division identified below. The petition must include proof of your ownership interest in the property or proof that you were a victim of the offense underlying the pending forfeiture, or a related offense, and the facts and circumstances which you believe justify a return of the property, a return of your interest in the property, or a return of part of the property. For the regulations pertaining to remission or mitigation of the forfeiture see 28 C.F.R. Sections 9.1-9.9. The criteria for requesting remission of the forfeiture are found at 28 C.F.R. Section 9.5(a). The criteria for requesting mitigation of the forfeiture are found at 28 C.F.R. Section 9.5(b). You should file the petition within thirty (30) days following the receipt of this mailed notice of seizure.

Where to Submit Correspondence

The Seizure Number 3540020033 has been assigned to this forfeiture action. Use this number to identify the property when submitting a claim, petition or other correspondence to the FBI.

Submit all documents to this FBI Field Division:

SPECIAL AGENT IN CHARGE
FEDERAL BUREAU OF INVESTIGATION
FAST
26 FEDERAL PLAZA, 28TH FLOOR
NEW YORK, NY 10278

ATTENTION: FORFEITURE PARALEGAL SPECIALIST
212-384-2899

Sincerely Yours,

Mark T. Ukleja
Unit Chief
Forfeiture and Seized Property Unit
Finance Division

NOTE: All telephone inquiries should be directed to the aforementioned FBI Field Division to the attention of the Forfeiture Paralegal Specialist. **Please do not send any written correspondence to Mark T. Ukleja.**

Sworn Statement of BR Shetty at American Embassy in Abu Dhabi

U.A.E. Exchange Centre, L.L.C.
By: Mr. B.R. Shetty
Title: Vice Chairman and Managing Director
  United Arab Emirates
State of Emirates of Abu Dhabi   )
  City of Abu Dhabi   )   ss.: SS
United Embassy of the United   )
  Arab Emirates   )
  States of America   )

U.A.E. Exchange Centre, L.L.C., by Mr. B.R. Shetty, being duly sworn, under oath and subject to the penalties of perjury, deposes and says:

I am the Vice Chairman and Managing Director of claimant described in the foregoing Notice of Claim. I have read the claim and know the contents thereof, and the same is true to my own knowledge, except as to matters therein stated to be upon information and belief, and as to those matters, I believe them to be true.

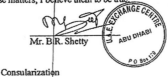

Mr. B.R. Shetty

Consularization

On **18 FEB 2002** before me, the undersigned, a _Vice Consul_ , personally appeared Mr. B.R. Shetty, personally-known-to -me-or proved to me on the basis of satisfactory evidence to be the individual(s) whose name(s) is (are) subscribed to the within instrument and acknowledged to me that he/she/they executed the same in his/her/their capacity(ies), and that by his/her/their signature(s) on the instrument, the individual(s), or the person upon behalf of which the individual(s) acted, executed the instrument.

Elizabeth E. Wilson
Vice Consul of the
United States of America
Consular Official

Later on Sultan Suwedi, had told the authorities that the prime 9/11 suspects, referred to as the ring-leaders by US authorities, were banking in the UAE - Atta's bank account with a top international bank had a lot of traffic and Marwan who was banking with HSBC in UAE had comparatively little traffic in his account. Suwedi had further said that US investigators would get a good lead from the review of these accounts. Sultan was himself handling these two accounts for the ring leaders.

After picking up the 9/11 connections, we had decided that our report would recommend that the exchange should change its name. We also took note that their US-based lawyers were using "UAE" as a short name in their correspondence and which was actually tarnishing the country's reputation.

One interesting event happened during the examination. A friend of Wahab dropped in at the Exchange's branch in Deira Dubai to deliver a letter to him and casually inquired whether the UAE Exchange was a sister company of UAE Central Bank. Wahab clarified that it was not and that two private individuals with no UAE government connection owned the exchange. The acting branch manager of the exchange was incidentally present and we realized that a common man was being misguided completely by the name. We had therefore in our audit report recommended that the exchange should change its name and our department, based on the reviewers endorsement to our recommendation, seconded the report for the Governor's approval.

There is a unique corruption at the UAE Central Bank. Some employees misuse their position to obtain lucrative jobs for their relatives in financial institutions they are dealing with in the course of their functions. I know of various examiners, using their influence, obtained lucrative jobs for their spouse, brother, son or daughter. They soon become tools in the hands of those entities and I have seen them compromising on various fronts. Some become active spies for those institutions. One such parasite passed on the information to the management of UAE Exchange Centre that I had recommended the change of name and that the Executive Director had endorsed the report and passed it over to the Governor for his decision.

One fine morning Saeed's secretary informed me that the Governor wanted to see me and Saeed immediately. No sooner had we entered Suweidi's office than he told us that B R Shetty had complained that I had passed over FBI Seizure documents to the Chairman of Andhra Bank in India and immediately suspended me from conducting any audits. Suweidi runs Central Bank like a dictator. No suspension memo was given to me nor the matter passed over to the Disciplinary Committee for investigation and I was suspended without even being given an opportunity to be heard. Saeed was visibly upset that his golden boy was grounded, but he was helpless in front of the powerful Governor.

Later in the day around 10 o'clock or so, B R Shetty and his shadow Sudhir Shetty came to meet Saeed. They complained that I had faxed seizure documents to the Chairman of Canara Bank. I immediately sought clarification that the Governor referred Andhra Bank, but Saeed cut me off and said that maybe the Governor might have made a mistake.

I inquired with Shetty as to why I would harm him since I had no enmity with his exchange. B R Shetty, promised to come back within three days with concrete evidence from the telecom company (Etisalat, which is the only telecom company operating in the UAE) linking the faxes sent to my telephones. Saeed noted that after a week, Shetty should come back with evidence from the telephone company.

Those seven days passed like seven years and my suspension was slowly becoming the gossip at the Central

Bank. Shetty did not come back and my suspension continued up to twenty-one days.

During this period, Wahab was on leave and as soon as he resumed duty, he approached Saeed supporting me and explaining to Saeed that it was a ploy to sidetrack our recommendation demanding that the exchange change its name. Audit partners like Wahab are a rarity and my relationship with him was further bonded.

Those three weeks are perhaps the most unpleasant days of my life, which I will never forget. I have a passion for two things in my life; one is Cricket and the other to watch Indian Hindi movies. My situation in those days, resembled a character played by Anil Kapoor in the movie "PUKAR", where he was framed and suspended from his duties. The whole world was gunning for his head and his boss who believed in him was helpless, like Saeed in my case. The movie eventually fetched him a national award.

I don't know whether it was a ploy or that the exchange was really a victim of abuse by somebody, but the suspension broke my heart and I had decided that I would leave Central Bank. I was thinking about taking legal action against B R Shetty and his Exchange but I had no proof of my suspension. Further, the 9/11 issues were very sensitive ones and I could have been easily wiped out in the UAE or perhaps thrown into jail.

In mid-2004, B. R. Shetty, who was now the Chairman of Abu Dhabi Cricket Council announced that the inaugural match at the new Abu Dhabi Cricket stadium would kick start with a one day cricket match between arch rivals India and Pakistan. At a press conference, the date of the match was announced with a lot of pomp.

An India vs. Pakistan cricket match is a big money spinner and evokes tremendous international response. The Indian Board did not give its blessings or approval to release the current Indian Cricketers, because of "Match Fixing" fears and the proposed match had to be cancelled. I did read in the newspapers that Shetty made valiant trips in India to pull strings, but in the end had to eat humble pie.

In May 2005, Shetty finally managed to organize a cricket tournament in Abu Dhabi, taking the cover of Tsunami disaster. Up to now the connection between the great game of cricket to 9/11 was very thin – The cricket matches generally start at 9 o' clock and the two participating teams have 11 players on their side. But with Shetty, heading the Abu Dhabi Cricket Society and the participating Indian, Pakistani and Sri Lankan players wearing shirts with the logo of UAE Exchange Centre, the bond between cricket and 9/11 has become stronger and more permanent.

It is an apt lesson to ICC, the worldwide governing body for the game, to verify the credentials of the organizers and sponsors before giving the nod to any cricket tournaments in any part of the globe. Cricket is a gentlemen's game and should be run by people with impeccable reputation.

As per reports reaching me, Shetty recently fired his long time senior manager, accusing him of leaking documents pertaining to 9/11 episode to various banks in India. His devilish brain it seems has run out of ideas.

In early 1996 the Narcotics wing of the UAE Police approached the UAE Central Bank to investigate money laundered by Vicky Goswami, who was operating a drug factory in the Emirates. The investigative team comprised some big names at the Central Bank – Farooq Amin Ashraf, Salim Mushtaq and Khamis Bu Haroon. I do not know in detail what was the observation of the investigating team, all I know is that Farooq, a very dedicated senior auditor , who was heading the examination team had added one more enemy to his list.

Unfortunately in the audit profession, an honest auditor makes more enemies than friends. Everybody at the Central Bank was aware about the end results of the investigation but as usual the Governor closed the lid. Per press reports Goswami , who had strong ties to the Mafia, had earlier fled from South Africa (wanted by the South African police) to set up a base in UAE, was later named as a prime suspect in the sensational murder of Indian music baron, Gulshan Kumar. Per Indian Police it was a contract killing (Supari – as it is called in the mafia terminology).

As the story goes, after his release from UAE Prison, Goswami was mysteriously murdered and the Indian Police have not been able to solve the murder mystery of this saint music guru but now they have some lead in the right direction of approaching the Central Bank and obtain the trail of remittance moving from Goswami .

Just prior to his death, the late ruler of UAE, Sheikh Zayed felicitated, Shetty for his valuable contribution to the UAE economy. I do not know whether Zayed was aware about the seizure of UAE's Exchanges bank account in New York in connection with the 9/11 terror attack but then a rose is always surrounded with lot of thorns.

ADCB – HSBC
CONNECTION

The Abu Dhabi Government owns Abu Dhabi
Commercial Bank and Suweidi ran the bank prior to
joining the Central Bank. Suweidi has a unique quality of
keeping wrong people at wrong places like placing round
pegs in square holes. A bird once told me that the Head of
Loans & Advances at ADCB was earlier heading the
Stationery Department. The Chief Auditor has no
accounting background (and rejects qualified CPA's who
are interviewed by him to join the audit department), while
the head of Credit Card operations, who is a qualified
accountant, is wasted.

The highly talented former General Manager,
Andersen, who formerly was the head of ANZ Grindlays
Asian Operations was sidelined completed during
Suweidi's tenure at ADCB.

My last examination of ADCB was a very
memorable one for I picked up various controversial issues
notably the controversial bank accounts opened on the
instructions of a top member of the Ruling Family. The
Wall Street Journal report (dated September 17,2003) on

these dirty accounts was based on my memo to Suweidi. I am not aware whether the US Regulators did take any action against ADCB. In my opinion ADCB's US bank account should be investigated as the funds which were denominated in US dollars were routed through USA and the US Banking System was abused. A detailed trail of the funds would definitely answer the question, who were the end beneficiaries? Or were they related to any terrorist activities?

These accounts were opened with ADCB's Main Branch and I went to discuss them with the Branch Manager. By a coincidence one of their Internal Auditor's was also present and the first thing he asked me – "How did you pick them so soon? They are money laundering accounts but don't tell Suweidi I told you."

The Branch Manager who is a UAE National went on to add that there are only two intelligent auditors in the Central Bank – one is Farooq and the other you.

The entire senior management of ADCB was dumbfounded when I showed them the bank account of Credit Commercial de France, a subsidiary of HSBC. The account was denominated in the UAE Dirham, the local currency of UAE and I was surprised why it was not opened with any of the HSBC's branches in the UAE but opened at ADCB, a competitor bank. A review of the account showed substantial incoming funds was immediately routed out ranging from AED 290,000 to AED 93.4 million.

The funds were not linked to any oil transaction or any Government contract. ADCB management was clueless on the nature of these transactions and could not forward any explanations.

I immediately faxed a memo to Saeed, who passed it to the Reviewer in charge of HSBC bank. The Reviewer after discussing the accounts with HSBC (I am not aware about his discussion with HSBC) forwarded to Saaed with his comments and Saeed in turn passed it to Suweidi. I am sure Suweidi must have forwarded the memo to his "Pending Tray".

In mid 2003 officers of Homeland Security in New York, who were passed a copy of the account statement by WSJ on my behalf did confirm to me in a meeting in their office that the account shows a money-laundering pattern. I have also passed on a copy of this account to KPMG the worldwide auditors of HSBC recently but I know the general public will never come to know – were they tainted? Or terrorist related funds?

HSBC has recently agreed to US Regulators that ten wire transfers were sent from Riggs Bank in USA to Credit Commercial De France (a subsidiary of HSBC) in Luxembourg and HSBC in Luxembourg aggregating to US Dollars 8.1 million from E G oil account to Apexside Trading banking with IISBC - You see 9 of these wire transfers were through Credit Commercial De France – The bank at the centre of my concern in ADCB.

Correspondent accounts can be easily misused and bankers should always keep an eye on them all the time and in my opinion are like a time bomb ready to explode any time.

Abu Dhabi Commercial Bank
═══ *Statement Inquiry* ═══

Date:19/03/02   Page: 1/8

Account Number : 1905800045   CREDIT COMMERCIAL DE FRANCE

Date	Description	Debit	Credit	Balance
30/12/00	BROUGHT FORWARD			219,604.200
04/01/01	INWARD TT			
	HSBC ME DXB V 0401	-	4,435,700.000	4,655,304.200
04/01/01	INWARD TT			
	ABN. AMRO BK DUBAI V 04		4,493,642.000	9,148,946.200
04/01/01	INWARD TT			
	B/O HSBC ME DXB V 04		5,131,473.000	14,280,419.200
04/01/01	INWARD TT			
	ABN AMRO BK DUBAI V 04		8,240,172.000	22,520,591.200
04/01/01	INWARD TT			
	HSBC ME DXB V 04		15,463,560.000	37,984,151.200
04/01/01	INWARD TT			
	ABN AMRO BK DUBAI V 04		42,533,251.990	80,517,403.190
04/01/01	OTHERS			
	AGEI P3014 V 04	4,435,745.000		76,081,658.190
04/01/01	OTHERS			
	TD SAT 3362880 V 04	4,493,687.000		71,587,971.190
04/01/01	OTHERS			
	AGEI P3014 V 04	5,131,518.000		66,456,453.190
04/01/01	OTHERS			
	TD SAT 3362874 V 04	8,240,217.000		58,216,236.190
04/01/01	OTHERS			
	AGEI P 3014 V 04	15,463,605.000		42,752,631.190
04/01/01	OTHERS			
	TD SAT 3362869 V 04	42,533,297.000		219,334.190
11/01/01	INWARD TT			
	SPTMID090830		3,700,000.000	3,919,334.190
11/01/01	OTHERS			
	AGEI P3014 11/1	3,700,045.000		219,289.190
13/01/01	INWARD TT			
	FWDMID100076		11,126,030.130	11,345,319.320
13/01/01	OTHERS			
	TD/TAT 3367939 12/1	11,126,075.000		219,244.320
05/02/01	INWARD TT			
	FWDMID020956		4,493,642.000	4,712,886.320
05/02/01	OTHERS			
	AGE P3077 5/2	4,493,687.000		219,199.320
14/02/01	DRAFT ISSUED			
	CSH ORDER 1045601229	2,400.000		216,799.320
26/02/01	INWARD TT			
	FWDMID021016		42,533,252.000	42,750,051.320
	CONTINUED...			

More Pages: 1 2 3 4 5 6 7 8

Account History	Statement	Guarantors	Guarantees	Fin. Transactions	Non-fin. Transactions

Correspondent bank account of HSBC's subsidiary at ADCB

Abu Dhabi Commercial Bank
═══ *Statement Inquiry* ═══

Date:19/03/02   Page: 2/8
Account Number : 1905800045   CREDIT COMMERCIAL DE FRANCE

Date	Description	Debit	Credit	Balance
26/02/01	BROUGHT FORWARD			42,750,051.320
26/02/01	INWARD TT			
	733010221500046		93,351,139.880	136,101,191.200
26/02/01	OTHERS			
	AGEIP3118 26/2	42,533,287.000		93,567,904.200
26/02/01	OTHERS			
	TD/TAT3392790 26/2	93,343,556.000		224,348.200
27/02/01	OTHERS			
	TD/A3394170 27/2	290,168.000		-65,819.800
28/02/01	INWARD TT			
	AM 032		290,133.030	224,313.230
28/02/01	INTEREST CHARGED	50.000		224,263.230
08/03/01	DRAFT ISSUED			
	CSH ORDER 1066012371	2,300.000		221,963.230
12/03/01	INWARD TT			
	REF 3106113015		7,222,801.060	7,444,764.290
12/03/01	OTHERS			
	TD/A3397714 12/3	7,222,836.000		221,928.290
04/04/01	INWARD TT			
	REF DPS		65,000.000	286,928.290
04/04/01	INWARD TT			
	733010331500214		4,435,700.000	4,722,628.290
04/04/01	INWARD TT			
.	B/O ABN DXB		5,131,472.990	9,854,101.280
04/04/01	OTHERS			
	TD TSVT 3414667 4/4	4,435,735.000		5,418,366.280
04/04/01	OTHERS			
	TD/TSVT 3414665 4/4	5,131,508.000		286,858.280
11/04/01	INWARD TT			
	B/O ABN DXB		3,700,000.020	3,986,858.300
11/04/01	OTHERS			
	TD /TSVT 3418317 11/4	3,700,035.000		286,823.300
19/04/01	INWARD TT			
	733010419500007		3,700,000.000	3,986,823.300
19/04/01	INWARD TT			
	7330104195 00005		5,079,815.010	9,066,638.310
19/04/01	OTHERS			
	TD SAT 3422578 19/4	3,700,035.000		5,366,603.310
19/04/01	OTHERS			
	TD/SAT3422576 19/4	5,079,850.000·		286,753.310
	CONTINUED...			

More Pages: 1 2 3 4 5 6 7 8

Account History	Statement	Guarantors	Guarantees	Fin. Transactions	Non-fin. Transactions

Correspondent bank account of HSBC's subsidiary at ADCB

Abu Dhabi Commercial Bank
═══ *Statement Inquiry* ═══

Date: 19/03/02   Page: 3/8

Account Number : 1905800045   CREDIT COMMERCIAL DE FRANCE

Date	Description	Debit	Credit	Balance
19/04/01	BROUGHT FORWARD			286,753.310
19/04/01	OTHERS			
	TD/SAT3422573 19/4	18,940,240.000		-18,653,486.690
21/04/01	INWARD TT			
	7330104195 00006		18,940,205.000	286,718.310
25/04/01	INWARD TT			
	SPTMID139936		5,870,342.000	6,157,060.310
25/04/01	OTHERS			
	AGEI P3014 25/4	5,870,377.000		286,683.310
30/04/01	INTEREST CHARGED	15,026.120		271,657.190
02/05/01	INWARD TT			
	FWDMID179905		3,700,000.000	3,971,657.190
02/05/01	OTHERS			
	AGEI P3014 2/5	3,700,035.000		271,622.190
07/05/01	INWARD TT			
	SPTMID230787		4,286,951.000	4,558,573.190
07/05/01	OTHERS			
	AGEI P 3014 7/5	4,286,986.000		271,587.190
09/05/01	INWARD TT			
	FWDIMID029939		8,240,172.000	8,511,759.190
09/05/01	TELEX TRF			
	6001050255 AED0240172	8,240,207.000		271,552.190
15/05/01	INWARD TT			
	SPTMID311264		1,100,000.000	1,371,552.190
15/05/01	OTHERS			
	AGEIP3014 15/5	1,100,035.000		271,517.190
16/05/01	DRAFT ISSUED			
	CSH ORDER 1136603788	13,800.000		257,717.190
29/05/01	INWARD TT			
	B/O HSBC DXB		3,700,000.000	3,957,717.190
29/05/01	INWARD TT			
	B/O HSBC DXB		12,022,278.000	15,979,995.190
29/05/01	INWARD TT			
	B/O HSBC DXB		50,476,176.000	66,456,171.190
29/05/01	OTHERS			
	AGEI P3014 29/5	3,700,000.000		62,756,171.190
29/05/01	OTHERS			
	AGEI P3014 29/5	12,022,313.000		50,733,858.190
29/05/01	INWARD TT			
	RV6148090032 29/5	50,476,176.000		257,682.190
	CONTINUED...			

More Pages: 1 2 3 4 5 6 7 8

Account History	Statement	Guarantors	Guarantees	Fin. Transactions	Non-fin. Transactions

THE LAUNDERING PRINCE

The spider web also spread to Abu Dhabi Commercial Bank and at the center was the Prince introducing three accounts, using his clout, which was picked up by me while examining a large transactions report, generated internally by every bank for management's review. I had a difficult time getting the files and had to meet the head of their private banking unit, who very reluctantly gave me the files for two accounts – Pennand, Inc. and Tiberius Limited.

He commented that the file for a third one, Devonia Investments, was handled by the Managing Director of the bank personally. A brief on the two accounts reviewed by me is given below and should find a permanent place on the website of Financial Action Task Force, the international body reviewing money laundering transactions around the globe, as a classic example of money laundering.

Pennand, Inc.: A company incorporated in Liberia with 500 bearer shares without par values. The bank account was operated by Peter Bond (British), Christopher

Samuelson (British), Ruslan Fomichev (Russian) and Joseph Kay (American).

As per the standing instructions, 4% of the total amount received was to be transferred on the 15th and 30th day of each month to Sopton Trading, maintaining a bank account with Banque SCS Alliance in Geneva and another 4% to Tiberius Limited, banking with Curaco International Bank, NV.

Based on the review of the Call account maintained in US dollars, regular inward remittance from Cherrylane GR, and Cremona Financial Corp were seen ranging from US $1 million to US $24.7 million, nearly all of which was transferred out.

Tiberius Limited: A company incorporated in Isle of Man with a share capital of Sterling 2000 only. The same persons operating Pennand, Inc. were also the authorized signatories for US dollar Call and Fixed Deposit accounts and the account had similar standing instructions to transfer funds like Pennand, Inc.

The account which was opened on October 10, 2000 received incoming remittance aggregating US $65.7 million from Cherrylane and Cremona, of which USD $49.6 million was transferred to Fixed Deposit account and later on practically everything was moved out.

I was told that based on a query received from Sultan Suweidi, all information pertaining to Devonia Investments was forwarded to the Central Bank. Apparently, some international agencies were already investigating this one. The Wall Street Journal reported this web of accounts and in response to their query, Nariman, the Beauty Queen of the Central Bank, replied that these accounts were discussed with the management of ADCB and closed by the bank, but not because of any money laundering issues. The beauty Queen's brain has rusted over the years spent in the corridors of the Central Bank

Why were the funds there in the first place, in the UAE?

She avoided the question about the Prince's connection altogether. Reports indicate Bond and Samuelson ran the Valmet Group from the Isle of Man and were involved in setting up dummy companies for their clients, including providing an address and nominee directors for the shell companies formed by them.

In a US Court, Bond had admitted setting up 30 dummy companies for Robert Brennan (a controversial stock promoter now serving a long prison term in the USA for defrauding investors). In exchange for his testimony against Brennan, the US authorities granted Bond immunity and he thus escaped the prison sentence.

Interestingly, the duo had a third friend named Stephen Curtis, a British lawyer who led a lavish lifestyle and had good Russian connections. Stephen was mysteriously killed in a helicopter crash in March 2004 after tipping off UK's National Criminal Intelligence Service about illicit Russian business activities. A couple of years earlier, the Spider Web scandal had claimed its first victim, a top US banker reported to be one of the richest men in his time, and having Middle Eastern origins, but popularly called the Golden Man, because of his appetite for the yellow metal.

The banker, who also owned a US bank and reportedly had excellent Russian contacts, was mysteriously finished off. I am glad that my partner Obaid and his family were not at their villa in Sharjah when the Russian mafia attacked his house.

I could not find any dossiers on the Russian and the American who were also named as authorized signatories. The Russian perhaps was a chairman of a private Russian bank. The international authorities should investigate these three bank accounts, the trail of which can be found by reviewing the correspondent bank account of

ADCB, maintained in the USA. The billion dollar question is where did the funds come from and who were the end beneficiaries? Mafia or terrorists or some politicians?

I have written to the Financial Action Task Force and to the UK Government to investigate this crime and ensure that criminals are forced to face the music.

On these accounts, my favorite Indian cricket commentator would have commented on the following lines, "Princes are like toilets, flush some days but broke most days."

My other favorite cricket personality from Yorkshire would have commented similarly, "Lollipop decision for the umpire, even my sister would not hesitate to call the Prince out."

LAST MEETING WITH SUWEIDI

As I had already decided following the UAE Exchange episode that I would be leaving Abu Dhabi, I had made up my mind not take a back seat in my meeting with Suweidi, but I certainly did not know that this meeting with the Governor in October 2002 would be the last one. As soon as I entered his room, he stood up shook my hands and said, "Hello, Revenge Man."

To which I replied, "Why are you again calling me the Revenge Man?"

He said, "Because of the HSBC allegation."

I shot back, "You are fully aware of HSBC's activities."

Suweidi got a bit angry and said, "You mean John Bond is a launderer?"

I did not reply to his question and I leave it to John Bond to answer. But I reminded him of David Bagley's memo to his bosses in London, admitting money laundering. He said, "As far as my memory goes, there was no such memo at all," and he commented that he had a strong memory.

I was in no mood to give in to him, as the UAE Exchange suspension was fresh in my mind, and replied that my memory was equally good and I promised to send him a copy of the memo.

I told him that lately I had picked up various issues at ADCB. Three fraud cases, an ADNIC letter of awareness case, and Emirates Palomar and Algerian documentary collection-related money laundering. Were they all revenge related cases?

Suweidi just stared at me and I can tell you must be admiring my guts. I told him point blank that I was a straightforward man and do not believe in buttering up anyone. I hope Suweidi recalls my words, which he must have felt were bitter, but truth usually is.

Suweidi inquired about the reason of my visit and I handed him two memos, one for upgrading my grade in line with Central Bank rules to Special Grade and the other three months of unpaid leave on emergency grounds. Suweidi replied that he needed a week to decide and asked me to follow up with his secretary.

I left, and I remember he did not extend his hand for the customary shake hand. I was back in ten minutes with Bagley's historical memo, as I wanted to further put Suweidi in a tight corner, but he told his secretary that he was busy and to collect it from me. I did not have the pleasure of seeing his face turning pale, but I can tell you that Suweidi must have realized that I was a fearless lion, prepared to tear him apart verbally, and must have decided not to meet me again that day.

Let me tell you, friends, that this is a fair and correct description of what transpired at that meeting and not a single word is spiced. Suweidi, do you remember? But unfortunately his memory is not as sharp as mine and to make him recollect the meeting, the said memo of Bagley is attached. I am confident that the memo will haunt him day and night for the rest of his life.

Don't worry my friends, Suweidi is a thick-skinned shameless person and will not end his life, but will continue to live a life of disgrace.

I had written a lovely poem with the title –"Do you remember" to my wife and which is reproduced below:

DO YOU REMEMBER

Do you remember?
When we first met
Our eyes were set
Our hands met
Our lips fret
Your breath I smelt
And our bodies melt
Our first glance
Resulting in our wedding dance
Our first date
Together we ate our wedding cake
Do you remember our romantic honeymoon?
So why fight? Let's repeat it soon.

Suweidi will always remember me up to his last breath and my fight with him will continue because it is the fight against injustice, an uprising against institutions involved in dirty money and terrorist accounts.

I had thrown a farewell party to some of my friends at my home on September 15, 2002, which coincided with the birthday party of my son, Asif. I had indicated to them that I would be leaving UAE, because there was a threat to my life if I continued living here as I had made influential persons my enemies. But the surprise guest of the evening was Abu Nasr, who had been transferred from Abu Dhabi to Dubai. Actually we were in the middle of the party when Nasr rang up on my mobile phone and announced that he was visiting Abu Dhabi. I immediately invited him to join us for the Biryani (spicy rice cooked with meat).

Despite staying in Abu Dhabi for more than five years Nasr had never visited my house. This was his first and last visit. I still remember his words as if it was uttered just yesterday, Nasr said, "I am coming over to meet your dear mother and not for Biryani." His words, which came straight from his heart, once again touched me.

My friends Azhar, Mustafa, Hassan Ali, Haroon and Naeem attended the historic party among others, and it was captured on my video camera. The very next day Azhar hosted a farewell party in my honor.

I followed up with Suweidi's secretary, who after confirming with him, called to inform me that the leave was approved but the grade change memo was rejected. I had decided that I would be utilizing the leave period to explore alternative employment opportunities. After all it would be foolhardy to tender resignation without first having a source of income, because along with your ethics one also has a belly to fill and bills to pay to support a family, but leaving UAE was a certainty, only on my terms and at the proper time.

TIT FOR TAT REPLY

One of the greatest mistakes Suweidi made in his life was to half-way terminate my contract with the reason, "Did not return to work even after one month from the date of his approved leave." Someone at the Personnel Department summoned my housekeeper, who took care of my family, telling her to vacate the bank's accommodation as quickly as possible, as my contract was terminated.

I am a human being and shot off a strongly worded letter to Suweidi and demanded compensation for discrimination, wrongful termination, and racial abuse, failing which I would take up the matter with the appropriate authorities. In the letter I had told him that this time he has crossed the wrong man.

The next day, Saeed rang me up, but his trembling voice gave the impression that he was very nervous. The first thing he said was, "We are all going to lose our jobs."

I replied, "I have already lost mine."

He persuaded me to forgive and forget the matter and not to go ahead with my action. He was shocked that I referred the Central Bank as a Whorehouse. I told him to check up that matter with Sinkas and Saleh Alawi, the

Senior Manager and Manager respectively, of the Department.

Saeed, who had always been my strong supporter, lost his cool and said, "We will get you by hook or by crook from India."

Afterwards, the Deputy Governor rang me up to lure me into coming back to Abu Dhabi, promising me whatever position I desire. I declined immediately and dispatched to him a thank you letter. The offer could have been a trap to call me to Abu Dhabi and put me behind bars forever. I then sent a strongly worded complaint letter to various authorities in the UAE, including the Ruling Family, seeking justice and also pointed out the massive money laundering operations I had picked up.

I also approached the Indian Ambassador in Abu Dhabi seeking his assistance and spent a fortune calling Abu Dhabi to speak to him, but could only speak to his secretary, who stated that the Embassy had no jurisdiction over it as the case was very sensitive and suggested that I approach the Indian Ambassador in Washington.

I contacted The Indian Ambassador in Washington, but no help was forthcoming, except that one of his assistants called up and I faxed him documents showing the massive money laundering I had unearthed, including one big scam originating from a top Indian bank in Calcutta, involving millions and millions of dollars.

Suweidi had the support of the influential members of the Royal Family involved in laundering millions through ADCB, and managed to keep his job. To show his authority, he issued a circular against me to all banks operating in the UAE, and also instructed them to display the same on the notice boards of all their branches.

CENTRAL BANK OF THE U.A.E.

Notice No.	:	1254/2003
DATE	:	/05/2003
To	:	All Banks & Moneychangers
Sub	:	Central Bank's Ex-employee Mr. Iqbal Ismail Hakim

After greetings,

Please be advised that the services of the Central Bank employee, Mr. Iqbal Ismail Hakim, of Indian nationality, holder of passport No- E-1575756 was terminated WEF 16/12/2002, due to his failure to report to work after more than one month from the end of his leave. The said person used to hold the position of " Chief Examination Officer".

Accordingly, the relation of the above mentioned person with the Central Bank has ceased with effect from date of termination of his services. You are therfore requested not to provide him with any data or information of any sort, under any capacity whatsoever. The Central Bank shall not be responsible for any dealings with the said person.

Please note that the mentioned person is now in the United States of America (New Jersy) and has started sending letters containing some allegations and fabrications relating to some banks and moneychangers in addition to the Central Bank, which are baseless.

Yours faithfully,

Sultan Bin Nasser Al Suwaidi
Governor

I became the talk of the town and one of my well-wishers forwarded the circular to me. I was not going to take any more nonsense from Suweidi and immediately sent a reply circular to all the banks in UAE explaining the issues picked up at HSBC Middle East and at UAE Exchange Centre, and that gave me a lot of relief. It was a tit for tat reply.

To: ALL BANKS & FINANCIAL INSTITUTIONS IN THE WORLD
FROM   : IQBAL ISMAIL HAKIM
SUBJECT : SULTAN SUWEIDI – GOVERNOR OF UAE CENTRAL BANK
          RESPONSE TO NOTICE NO 1254/2003 dated 4 May 2003

My contract was illegally terminated by him (when I was on an exceptionally long
unpaid leave) since I knew too much about his dirty financial system. My
Housekeeper managing my house and my three school going children in Abu Dhabi
were threatened to leave UAE in seven days or face eviction from the Bank's
accommodation. My three school going children lost one year of schooling as they
could not take the final exam. My new fourwheel drive mortgaged to the Central
bank was forcibly taken over at a throwaway price. My dues have not been fully
settled. The letters which the above notice refers are reminders to him and to the
various Government Authorities to settle my dues & my claim for damages.

I recently received a phone call from Mr Saeed Hamiz (Executive Director of the
Banking & Supervision department) threatening me of dire consequences followed
by another call by The Deputy Governor apologizing for the Central Bank's
mistakes and offering me a very senior post. I have turned down his offer. Suwedi
speak up, it this Fabrication ? If I am dishonest why threats are being made or re-
employment offered. My aim in life is to expose Suweidi to the world until he is sacked
from the Central bank. Here is the first one & the next one will be on a popular
Exchange.

He has let down the entire banking world, by mid way stopping the examination of
a top bank which admitted to laundering of millions of Dollars from Russia / CIS
countries from their Sharjah & Deira Branches. I led a team of 20 examiners and a
drama was created by him but he did not take any action against that Bank.
Suweidi, tell the World whether you are a
COWARD :FSA of UK threatened you to close the UK Branches of UAE
                      Banks in London ? OR
CORRUPT : The guilty Senior Management were allowed to leave UAE
                      Without any punishment WHY ?   OR BOTH
My audit partner Obaid Salami's house was attacked by the Russian Mafia
& I was accused of taking revenge and threatening the management. Obaid was so
scared that at the first available opportunity resigned from the Central bank.
It was also discovered that this bank was involved in financing oil transactions in
Violation of US/UN Sanctions, and other suspicious accounts.

Suweidi – Is this allegation or fabrication. If this is true then, SHUT UP
and spare the humiliation the UAE Banking will face because TRUTH
ALWAYS WINS IN THE END. I am a truthful person and You are the
biggest liar in the World.

People in the banking circles realized that I was
made a scapegoat by the Governor and evoked a lot of
sympathy for me and brick bats for Suweidi. This gave me
a lot of relief. The down-side was that I made HSBC and
UAE Exchange my sworn enemies.

CAPTAIN OF THE SINKING SHIP

I have never met Sir John Bond, the world renowned banker, who is the captain of the biggest bank in the UK, the Group Chairman, and at that time, the Chairman of HSBC Middle East Bank when they ran into a very straight forward honest regulator. The great Titanic ran into gigantic icebergs and sank deep into the ocean, never to return. HSBC will not sink and disappear into history like the Titanic, but its pride and reputation will sink to levels far lower than what can be measured by any instruments. Although I did not meet this icon I was impressed with his statement to the shareholders of HSBC Group in the 2003 Annual Report and I take pride in quoting him.

Sir John Bond wrote –"When I joined HSBC, to the best of my knowledge, we did not have a single regulator. Today we have over 370. In the final report, you cannot legislate trust and integrity. You cannot impose it. It comes from within."

Truly great words, but I would like to point out that HSBC executives stooped so far as to hit me below the belt, accused me of taking revenge, and changed my life completely.

Certainly HSBC does not want any regulators to regulate their misdeeds. Any infringement will be dealt with by an iron hand. They wield enormous power and can change the destiny of an ordinary man like me in minutes, but they cannot control everything to suit their books. People playing with fire one day get their own house burnt down.

A similar event happened with HSBC, they were bankers to arms dealers and terrorists and realized that the saying even holds true today. HSBC's Branch in Turkey was hit by a terrorist attack in 2003. My heart goes out to the families of the victims; some of them were staff of the bank.

I had written a poem, which is dedicated to countless victims falling to terrorist attacks every day around the globe lately. This is reproduced here:

The Love Culture

For many, life revolves only around money
Since it brings you closer to your honey
But if the honey is a victim of terror attack
You will eventually have a heart attack
The fear of Osama is everywhere
The world faces destruction everywhere
Life on the world started with Eve & Adam
At this rate, it will certainly end with the atom
The earth revolves around the sun
But life on earth revolves around the gun
Alas! There is no time for fun
I wish we all had a safe place to run
Next generation must not inherit gun culture
In their hearts, let us implant love culture

Love and only love should be at all places
This will make the world a safe place
Our lovely world started with Eve & Adam
Lets ensure it does not end with the atom.

I once again quote Sir John Bond, "What is important is the way a company behaves, at all levels. Words are not enough. Our reputation depends on deeds. HSBC will continue to expect the highest standards of behavior from its employees. And the Board, as your agents, will oversee your company to make sure that we continue to uphold our reputation. We will continue to aspire to the very highest standards."

I am really a fan of Sir John's words, but as he has commented, words are not enough. It has to be backed by deeds. I have done my bit and enlightened HSBC's Board of critical issues – some of them legal, some moral, some unethical and some illegal. It is a tradition that a captain of the ship has to go down with the ship and now I would like Sir Bond to take responsibility for the disasters at their Middle East operations.

Sir Bond should take a tip from Bagley, who had the guts to admit that they were launderer's, and like a gentleman, did not try to cover up the truth by a mountain of lies. Bond should come forward with facts and figures to explain the truth to the world.

I have officially complained to the UK regulators of HSBC, the Financial Service Authority, and they have advised that my complaint is being investigated. I have demanded that Sir Bond should graciously resign from the management, and HSBC Board should forward an unconditional apology to me. A letter to the Queen of England has also been sent with a request to withdraw the Knight's honor bestowed on Bond, should he refuse to take up the responsibility and resign like a gentleman.

My Yorkshire hero's comments would be something like this: Pressure Situation Here.

You see the Bond between the bat and a ball will bring pleasure, but a Bond between a banker and gangsters will bring pressure.

A BLACK CAMEL

After illegally terminating my contract, Sultan signed off an experience certificate letter stating that I was hardworking, honest and sincere but despite my departments objection refused to state my correct title of Chief Examination Officer in this testimonial letter, and instead used Senior Examiner. My identity card, visiting cards and even the circular letter, which he sent to the banking industry, referred me as a Chief Examination Officer.

Following the cancellation of my contract and the Wall Street Journal's article criticizing the UAE Central Bank, Sultan has been calling me a black sheep in his staff meetings, and the UAE Newspapers are often writing epic stories on my betrayals. Well Sultan, if I am a black sheep then let me bestow upon you a new title: You are a Black Camel of the Banking Industry.

Last year, the Highest Federal Auditing Authority in the UAE had criticized the UAE Central Bank, accusing it of suffering unnecessary losses, failing to fully undertake its role as a Government bank, indulging in practices that violate its founding rule, and its role as a credit supervisory body has remained incomplete. The state auditing office also bitterly accused the Central Bank of indulging in other malpractices, including the purchase of an electronic control system without signing a contract with the suppliers, and signing an agreement with a computer company and paying the first installment without receiving any guarantees from the computer company.

It will take me a complete book to spell out some of Suweidi's blunders, so I will name just a few:

A) Bank of Credit & Commerce International, BCCI as it was popularly known to the world, however after the collapse in the banking circles, people started calling it as the Bank of Criminals & Crooks International. The bank is still under liquidation for nearly fifteen years and was majority owned by the Ruler of Abu Dhabi .

I was the acting secretary to the UAE liquidators for two months during the absence of Salim Mushtaq (a seasoned banker) who is connected with the liquidation since it was transferred to the Central Bank. I understand small deposit holders with balances of UAE Dirham (UAE currency) 20,000 or less were settled in full. However large deposit holder's claims will never be paid in full.

In banking circles the talk was that the Ruler of Abu Dhabi, being the majority shareholder of BCCI, was compelled to fund the payout to the small depositors, which was routed through one of the relief agencies as a front. This was to avoid lawsuits being filed by the large deposit holders against the majority shareholder.

Despite being an over-banked country, nobody thinks about introducing the Depositors Protection Act and whenever there is a run on the banks, the Central Bank is compelled to come out with assurances and support.

The UAE did not deport two senior officers of BCCI based in the UAE and wanted by authorities all over the world on the pretext that they were being held in detention. Actually, they were given the princely treatment and were living in luxurious villas as state guests while serving their so called sentences. These two individuals, who are now on the payroll of an influential Royal family member, are enjoying life to the fullest in Abu Dhabi, and are ghost-running a bank and an exchange company. Legally no financial institutions can appoint them, as they are debarred from holding any position in view of their association with the fallen bank

B) Madhav Patel – The elusive Pied Piper. MP as I call him, continues to be untraceable and perhaps has become a fraud legend in the UAE banking circles. Imagine taking some seventeen banks for a jolly ride, hold your heart, aggregating to Dirhams one billion. A lot of bankers lost their jobs and the entire corporate team of a top international bank was sacked overnight.

The person who escaped scot-free instead of being sacked is Sultan Suweidi, the Governor of UAE Central Bank. The Risk Bureau Department, which processes a report on large borrowers in the UAE, was meant only for His Excellency's eyes, who in turn had delegated to one of his secretaries. Consequently, the huge exposure of Madhav Patel was never picked up at the Central Bank.

I took up the matter that a copy of this report covering large borrowers in UAE should be made available to each examiner for their noting. The then-manager of the Banking Supervision and Examination Department (BSED), Mohamed Sharif, who was a CPA, agreed with my views. Although my proposal was not accepted, at least now the Executive Director of BSED also gets a copy.

Following the MP scandal, the Chief of Dubai Police was highly vocal about Sultan's operational procedures. He suggested that the Inspectors at the police department did a better job than Sultan's men, and kept on attacking him at every opportunity. Sultan did not have the guts to take on the Dubai chief.

Some foreign banks operating in the UAE were very anxious to file suits against the Central Bank of the UAE for poor supervision but later decided that if you have to remain in Gulf waters, there is no point in making the alligator your enemy.

Interestingly, to review the Madhav Patel debacle, a team consisting of newly recruited European expatriates was selected by Suweidi and was headed by a Treasury Expert, while Patel's exposure to all banks was purely Unfunded – Acceptances. I received a call from one of the commercial bankers who was surprised that the Team Leader did not know the meaning of "Bill of Lading."

I am sure that bankers must have learned a lesson about getting reports from the International Maritime Bureau so as to verify trade related transactions of their customers. Interestingly the International Maritime Bureau had warned about Patel's fraudulent shipments, but nobody in the banking circles acted on this warning.

It seems MP has escaped into thin air. UAE authorities should think seriously since expatriate businessmen fleeing the country and leaving behind millions in debts is a chronic problem. MP actually is related to a top business family of India.

C) ISLAMIC BANK's Near Collapse Some years back, it was observed that there was a big hole in the assets of an Islamic bank, and the cause of this was never disclosed to the public. Public accountability, as a concept, is not in the dictionary of the UAE and it is high time that this was introduced statutorily, if UAE is to emerge as an important financial center.

It was no doubt a management fraud, however the story making rounds was that the bank management was a victim of a black magician, who promised to double the bank's money and hence they opened the bank's vault. He hypnotized them and disappeared with the cash booty. If this is true then, Allah save the banking world, because history repeats itself.

It should be a surprise to the world that when there was a crisis at this bank, the general public was forbidden to say anything about this episode- Absolutely no freedom of speech. I can imagine the depositors plight as the public in UAE were still recovering from the debacle of BCCI, which sank overnight, drowning millions of people around the globe, financially. The Central Bank did give assurance to the depositors, but their confidence in this Islamic bank was completely shattered, which actually gave birth to the formation of another Islamic Bank in the Emirates.

It was a disgrace that the big hole was not detected for some years by both the bank's Independent Auditors and the Central Bank Examiners. Later it was picked up by the Central Bank auditors while their independent auditors, one of the big accounting firms, was on the verge of signing a clean report.

D) A Bank dealing in its own shares. One of the smallest local banks in the UAE suddenly decided to show its power following the takeover by a prominent ruling family member as one of its new controlling shareholders. A bunch of young UAE national bankers took over the reins managing this bank and the results were disastrous.

A significant growth in lending was seen secured by local stocks/shares lending, including lending against its own shares, in contravention with the statutory regulations. This was picked up by the Central Bank Examiners and the Executive Director sought explanation from the erring bank. The young management sought to cover themselves by twisting the facts, and poisoned the ruling family shareholder.

The shareholder in question went after the Governor, who we understand was on vacation in

Switzerland and had to cut short his leave to appear before the influential shareholder.

To save his skin, the Governor apologized and fired the Executive Director. We were informed that the Executive Director had resigned after serving the Central Bank for more than two decades. I went to meet him in his office, and like a child, the Executive Director started crying and my heart went out to him.

Later, the cat was out of the bag and to sweeten the pot, the Governor proclaimed at the farewell party that his resignation was converted into a retirement by him with full retirement benefits. If you resign the retirement benefits are forfeited. The outgoing Executive Director once again broke down in tears and soon disappeared from the hastily arranged function at the meeting room of the Central Bank.

My parents had taught me that honesty is the best policy, but perhaps they were wrong and another honest person was slaughtered at the altar mercilessly but no sooner do you murder an honest soldier, another one appears to take his place.

A similar event occurred here with the Independent Auditors of the bank, qualifying their audit report citing that the bank was involved in dealing in their own shares. The honest auditors were dismissed at the next Annual General Meeting and another audit firm was appointed as the new auditors in their place.

The Governor handpicked Saeed Hamiz as the new Executive Director, and although an honest man, Saeed was actually a mere rubber stamp. His master's voice. Mohamed Sharif, who was the manager of the department, was overlooked and Sharif soon resigned from the Central Bank and joined another institution.

Later on, the bank management in question took a dig when the Central Bank examiners visited them and taunted that, "We got your Director fired."

E) Banker to Politicians Funds of an ex-ruler of a neighboring Gulf country running into millions of dollars are happily parked in one of the local banks and substantial lending is also done against these deposits. This is a smart way of managing funds since the loan taken is placed in another country. No questions were ever asked whether these funds actually belonged to the ruler or were siphoned off from the country's Treasury.

As the story goes, this ruler was away on holiday and in his absence, the son proclaimed himself as the new ruler. To his dismay, he found that the state treasury was virtually empty. The father had done some brilliant contingency planning by stashing a substantial chunk of the state funds in his personal bank account overseas.

It is a common knowledge that a former Prime Minister from the subcontinent is a popular guest of the UAE and by the grapevine, millions and millions of dollars acquired through bribes and kickbacks are invested in the Emirates in diversified ventures like real estate, exchange companies, gold, etc., using different people as frontmen.

These were reported to Sultan and must be lying in his pending tray

F) Timur – The Lame Duck of UAE A very popular figure in the UAE heads a controversial bank. At one point, his right hand man was more controversial than his boss, although I must admit, I liked his careless attitude. He was known as a Playboy in the banking circles. As the story goes, he would first taste the fruit before passing the same to his dear boss, may be to ensure that it is not a poisonous one.

The deputy was generally seen riding his Harley Davidson from time to time in the evening with a different companion every time, which made him the envy of all the men in the town. I once asked him about his rendezvous and he replied, "Who is not sleeping around in the banking world? I do it openly but not during the banking hours."

Lending to Directors of the bank has a lot of regulatory restrictions and the boss wanted to borrow substantial funds for his personal ventures from the bank. The Deputy came up with a brilliant idea to book the loan in the name of the boss's father and the father in turn to sign a Power of Attorney in favor of his son to operate the account. The loan eventually became a non performing one and after a few years the bank wanted to write off this loan, but the Governor's blessing was necessary.

The Governor agreed to give his blessing, but wanted to celebrate a second Bakri Idd in the same year. The Deputy was to become a sacrificial goat. It was an open secret that the deputy was never a favorite of the Governor, but because the Boss was a very powerful person from the Royal family, no one could touch his Man Friday. It was indeed sad that due to personal rivalry, the banking industry lost a good banker. He was instrumental in turning around the fortunes of this controversial bank, which is now limping very badly under the leadership of a new deputy.

Upon his arrival, the new deputy, a native from one of the Gulf countries, terminated most of the old boys and brought in a crew from his own country, which instantly became the talk of the town.

G) The Royal Kickback man. A grand old man closely connected to the Royal family, heads an important government organization. It is well known in town that for every project approved by him, a 20-25% kickback or commission is to be his share. The contractors are aware that this is the cost of doing business and it is actually factored into every quotation submitted to his organization.

Sizeable wealth has been accumulated in this manner in the last thirty years and the gentleman also owns various business ventures, which are heavily reliant on substantial loans from practically all the banks operating in the UAE.

As the story goes, his workers took him to court for non-payment of wages, and eventually the court issued a notice to the Central Bank to seize his bank accounts. Imagine the shock the Executive Director of the Banking Supervision and Examination Department of the Central Bank got when all the banks reported huge loans advanced to him and his companies, and only one reported a balance of less than a thousand dirhams (US $365 approx) in his favor. I am sure the funds must be safely tucked in banks outside the UAE so as not to attract the scrutiny of the Royal family.

Well, my dear readers, to keep the cat at an arm's length, a novel plan was hatched that the gentleman was cheated by some of his top managers running his business, whom he trusted blindly. The fraudulent managers had run up huge loans from various banks, without his knowledge or consent. Based on his complaint the police arrested two of his people and the Chief of the Central Bank was given an SOS message.

One of the greatest mistakes the Dictator of the Central Bank committed was:

He issued a directive to all the banks to immediately transfer bank balances of the disgraced employees and their family members to their master's account. A lot of bankers were astonished at this directive, which could only be issued by a court order.

He directed that all bank examiners investigate this fraud problem, leaving aside their present assignments. An interesting thought: If the Central Bank were to investigate frauds committed by employees, then the police would be unnecessary. Investigating frauds committed by the employees is certainly not a Central Bank function. Just to please the Royal old man, the Governor sent his men on a wild goose chase.

Eventually the gentleman would approach the top ruling member with his tale to seek financial assistance to settle the mammoth liabilities and in turn approach the lending banks to offer significant rebates to settle their exposures.

H) Import & Export of Large Currency Notes
Large inward currency notes do arrive in the UAE, either through passengers carrying it as baggage or through direct import by the exchange houses. The incoming currencies arriving in huge parcels are exported in the evening by exchange houses to banks in London. Day in and day out different currencies come in and go out aggregating to millions and millions of dollars. Some is converted into local dirhams and used to purchase gold, electronics, garments, cars, etc., while some is deposited into the banking sector to take advantage of the tax free system, and later wired out.

I remember the UK authorities were investigating a couple making significant trips between the UK and UAE and carrying suitcases full of cash to Dubai. The couple claimed they were buying Rado watches in Dubai. Converting dirty cash into valuable assets like gold, diamonds and expensive watches is one of the ways to clean dirty money. UAE's traders in the Gold Souk do not ask any questions and one can buy as much as one wants.

A very popular exchange, which according to the grapevine, was owned by an ex-politician from the subcontinent, saw its consignment of currency to the UK was frozen by the UK authorities. The exchange eventually ended up being liquidated.

A very small exchange house in Dubai frequently sends large currency notes to a neighboring country through a particular staff member. No fidelity insurance is held by that exchange and I will not be surprised if one day that staff member takes another flight and disappears putting another exchange into liquidation.

This was pointed out to the expatriate partner who commented that the staff member in question was his nephew and was hence trustworthy. The staff member in question has so many entry and exit stamps in his passport that will get him into trouble one day.

The banks in the UK, who in the past were buying tons of currency notes at a discounted price, have become very tough following 9/11 events on buying currency notes exported by the Gulf countries. As a grand gesture, the UAE Central Bank is buying currency notes in bulk from the Exchange Houses, which means that the UAE Central Bank is now officially a part of the Cleaning Industry.

The question is why tons of currency are allowed to come into this tiny country in the first place, when there are countless banks, which could be used to move funds. In today's world, tourists prefer to use plastic money and seldom carry substantial currency with them.

I) Large Non Resident Deposits. Most of the large international banks operating in the UAE have substantial non-resident deposits owned by foreign nationals not residing in the UAE. These are parked in the UAE for a couple of reasons, like tax free status, no questions being asked on the source of funds, no restrictions on repatriation of funds. The banks in question hardly have any background information on these depositors.

Some three years back a bank's officer noted that millions of dollars belonging to the notorious arms dealer Victor Bout (based on a Financial Times article) were parked in their Sharjah Branch. The senior management's attention was drawn and I know that the lady officer got herself into hot water. I distinctly remember shooting a memo to the Governor and recommending that his account should be frozen immediately and to this the Governor asked for three reasons.

Despite my giving six reasons to freeze these accounts, no action was ever taken and I do not know whether the funds are still parked in the UAE or adequate opportunity was given to move the funds out of the country. However I certainly do know that if the funds were frozen then a strong signal would have been sent to the launderers all over the world that they are not welcome here any more.

Let me also tell you that a lot of employee-related bank frauds involve non-resident deposits, because the bank staff is fully aware that the customer is not around, so these accounts are easy pickings.

J) Reserve Ratio Requirements All banks operating in the UAE are required to maintain a reserve ratio with the Central Bank for deposits accepted from the public. A top local Abu Dhabi bank openly flaunts this regulation. Large deposits are taken by the bank in the UAE, but only book entry is passed showing those deposits are a liability of its offshore Bahrain-based unit and therefore not within the jurisdiction of the UAE Central Bank. The funds are not remitted to Bahrain at all. Other banks are also in the process of emulating this bank. I am afraid this might be accepted as the industry's customary practice and there will hardly be any bank maintaining any banking reserve with the UAE Central Bank

K) Closure of Smith Barney Representative Office Last year, Sultan ordered the closure of Smith Barney's Representative Office for some stupid reason, but failed to take any action against HSBC, which had admitted indulging in money laundering, and violation of US/UN Sanctions, etc. It is a fact that following 9/11, the US authorities were coming down heavily on Sultan, and poor

Smith Barney was made the scapegoat. Sultan now has to justify to the world why no action was taken against HSBC.

L) Al Shiraee Marine Investment Company Fraud. Powerful Abu Dhabi locals duped a bunch of banks who had lent substantial funds to the above shell company based on the letter of awareness issued by a Government entity. Despite my reminders, Sultan just looked the other way and it is a mystery where the funds disappeared.

M) Post-Dated Checks & Personal Loans. Sultan has also failed to control the misuse of post-dated checks in the economy and is largely responsible for the sufferings of the common man in the UAE who have become easy prey to bankers offering liberal personal loans and credit cards, but charge huge interest rates with the result that the borrowers remain in debt for the rest of their lives.

N) Step-Motherly Treatment of Dubai. I cannot forget the statement made by Sultan when Sheikh Mohammed of Dubai launched the Dubai Financial City. Sultan did not support the idea and said, "It is the initiative of the Dubai Government and UAE Central Bank has nothing to do with it".

One prominent Director of the Central Bank who is a leading businessman in Dubai has also been at the receiving end when Sultan did not agree to approve his large exposure limit, while being very flexible to other directors from Abu Dhabi Emirate.

Sultan expected me to go down on my knees like one of the examiners did in the past, or cry like a baby which one of his former honest Executive Directors did, because they had no other alternative. But when I claimed compensation and damages I had clearly told him that, "This time you have crossed the wrong man."

Somebody had to attach a bell and put a chain on this black camel, which has lost his sense of direction and path. Yes, I have become a "Revenge Man," so the truth can come out, justice is served and criminals face the music. Yes my family and I have suffered a lot, and once I nearly thought of committing suicide by throwing myself in front of a running train.

But I didn't... I am still alive fighting against injustice and will continue to fight till my last breath.

PRE-9/11 WARNING FROM THE CENTRAL BANK OF SAUDI ARABIA

Months before the 9/11 terrorist attack, the Saudi Arabia Central Bank, Saudi Monetary Agency (SAMA), approached the UAE Central Bank forwarding a list of persons and organizations, receiving substantial incoming funds from Saudi Arabia.

SAMA wanted input from the UAE Central Bank on the beneficiaries who were banking with a popular Dubai based bank. The Governor did send a team to investigate and Obaid Salami was a part of the team. Obaid later disclosed to me that in his entire career he had never seen such substantial incoming transfers to personal accounts of individuals whose professions as stated in the bank records were salesman, cook or drivers.

The Governor did not forward any report to SAMA, but instead forwarded a copy of the bank statements for the parties identified by SAMA, as if to say "do your own homework." The Governor's reading of the issue was that it was Saudi's problem, since funds were originating from there and as such inquiries should be made by SAMA with the remitting bankers and their customers in Saudi Arabia.

SAMA came back strongly and returned the bank statements. This became a topic of intense discussion among bank examiners in Central Bank and it was a unanimous opinion of the Examiners that Sultan should not have forwarded the bank statements to a foreign Central Bank, as it amounted to breach of confidentiality. The constant reminders and follow-ups from SAMA, it seems, were consigned to Sultan's pending tray.

Some six months later, following the 9/11 event, with no response coming from Sultan, SAMA made a bold decision and black-listed the bank by issuing a circular to all banks operating in Saudi Arabia to sever all banking relations with said bank, and prohibited banks from any future dealings with that bank.

There was a panic in the UAE banking world as the news of the black-listing spread like a fire. Sultan then handpicked a close bunch of Arabic examiners to do a damage control exercise and write a favorable report for SAMA's consumption. Midnight oil burned at the Central Bank for nearly ten days as the Examiners got down to providing finishing touches on the monkey business.

Thereafter, using the Ruling family's contacts, a high level delegation was sent to meet the right persons in Saudi Arabia and by diplomatic pressure the ban on the bank was immediately lifted.

SAMA's concerns were dumped into the Arabian Sea. The 9/11 blame has been put solely on Saudi Arabia, while no fingers have been pointed at the UAE, which has escaped very easily despite the *known facts* that ring leaders of 9/11 banked in UAE; funds to the terrorists were transmitted from the UAE to the terrorist in the US; and the surplus funds in the possession of the terrorists were wired back from USA to institutions in the UAE for onward transferring to beneficiaries based in the UAE.

Authorities should approach SAMA and UAE Central Bank to solve this puzzle associated with the Dubai-based bank involved in the above controversy and who knows the trail may give valuable leads. I don't know whether or not the authorities have investigated the remitters and beneficiaries linked to the 9/11 terrorists and based in the UAE.

WHY BLAME
ARTHUR ANDERSEN?

I remember my teacher would always say, "Man is basically a greedy animal." I have now realized that practically every man in the world can be bought for a price and make him dance on your fingers if you have "Vitamin W2". Well, this is not a new drug, but the world's oldest medicine. Some sell their soul for 'Wealth,' but when wealth does not work, please pardon my bluntness, then try 'Women,' and sometimes both.

I had approached regulators (practically everybody), media (some of the top names in the industry), governments (US, UK, India, UAE), but none of them came to my rescue.

I don't know which "W" was used by the powerful institutions I had run into and in what doses, but I know they can afford both in large numbers.

In today's world, I am afraid there is no place for "Honesty" "Integrity" or "Ethics." Such words are meant only for the dictionary. In practical life, if you don't bend yourself to the situation or compromise, then your fate will be similar to mine, as both you and your entire family will suffer on all fronts, financially, emotionally and physically.

I have not seen my three kids and my mother for the last two years and it seems there is no end to my suffering. My telephones are tapped time and again; I am threatened by lawyers with dire consequences; followed by private detectives; my new Toyota Camry was deliberately stolen from New York as they thought that important documents were in the car; my wife was threatened by some Indian police officers and her baggage searched time and again; and she was shown a Red Arrest Warrant issued by UAE through INTERPOL.

The launderer's, fraudsters and other criminals continue to roam freely, instead of being behind bars, perhaps destroying the life of some other honest individual like me. Sometimes I wonder why blame Arthur Andersen, the auditors of Enron. They must have been under tremendous pressure from influential quarters to cover up Enron and must have buckled under pressure.

It is a very strange world. If you see something wrong and you keep quiet-people call you a coward. If you open your mouth, you lose your job. If you take up the matter with authorities, you are called a whistle-blower. If you don't take up the matter with the authorities, you may be charged as an accessory to a crime.

I happened to talk to a reporter who was in Dubai during the IMF and World Bank meeting and had approached Suweidi to seek his comments on the Wall Street Journal's article. Suweidi dismissed it as a baseless rumor. If that was baseless why did the UAE Central Bank, ADCB and HSBC not sue the newspaper for defamation, slander, and libel?

In my opinion, the little shepherd boy who cried 'wolf', grew up to become Sultan Suweidi. In the story, the shepherd boy was given a sound beating by the villagers for crying 'wolf' over and over.

Sultan Suweidi needs a similar thrashing by Banking Regulators from the USA, UK, India, Pakistan, Saudi Arabia and Algeria for misleading them and lying time and again that there is no money laundering or terrorist related funds in UAE. He should be brought to Ground Zero in New York and whipped in Islamic style. This would be an appropriate lesson to other Governors like him.

The least that the Financial Action Task Force (FATF) could do is to blacklist UAE immediately. Money laundering and Hawala trade is today second to none in the UAE, even perhaps beating the oil trade, and so lucrative that even the rulers have jumped on the band-wagon and are deeply into it. They should also investigate the bank accounts reported by me and I would not be surprised that most of them are terror-related in one way or another.

If Abraham Lincoln was alive today and saw as many dirty operations as I have seen and reported to Suweidi, he would have been tempted to describe UAE as a country of the launderers, for the launderers and by the launderers. The US regulators should also explain to the US banking industry why no action was taken against HSBC, and to the 9/11 victims why they did not raise their voice against Dubai holding the 58th Annual Meeting of the IMF and World Bank in September 2003, when they were fully aware that the prime 9/11 funding originated from Dubai and one of the ring leaders of 9/11 attack was a UAE national.

I am not a Mahatma Gandhi but my roots are from India and Indians don't give up easily, they fight till their last breath. I firmly believe in the traditional Sanskrit (the ancient Indian language) saying – Satya Mev Jayate, which means Truth Always Wins.

Incidentally, 9/11 is originally linked to the Great – Father of the Nation, as Indians affectionately refer him. Nearly one hundred years back on September 11, 1906

Gandhi-ji had launched his non-violence movement in South Africa and later on, even the British Government had no answer to his bloodless movement, which eventually won India its freedom.

Maybe the current terrorism problem the world faces can be solved the Mahatma way. The 9/11 event has wounded everybody, including the Muslim community, which actually has been the most affected by the 9/11 backlash.

Perhaps the long term solution to world wide terrorism, as President Mushraf, of Pakistan had recently stated, can be solved in a human way, "Find out why the terrorist or freedom fighter becomes so desperate that he becomes a human bomb and not only kills himself but also countless innocent people."

I am not a politician but like other common people would like terrorism to disappear from the world like the dinosaurs, and every possible solution should be tried by the world leaders so that peace returns to the land of Adam and Eve. The next generation should not inherit the gun culture. Let us implant the culture of love and tolerance. The lesson, "Live and let others live peacefully and happily" should be taught to them, right from birth.

As for myself, I know a bullet will be coming at me anytime, but if I keep quiet (which everybody advised me to do) I will be dying a thousand deaths every moment and I will fail in my own eyes. My courage to face the situation will give encouragement to honest auditors to do full justice to their profession, which of late has come under a lot of criticism.

My old mother who is waiting in India, whom I have not seen for the last two years, is always weeping whenever I speak to her on the phone. I have not visited India for various reasons like the Red Arrest warrant, the contract on my life, called "Supari," and my conscience to come clean with my family and friends that I am innocent. I was framed/blamed by powerful people of the bad wicked world. I know that one man alone cannot fight the corrupt system, but even the last flicker of the dying candle can burn the house.

I have left my country, India some 22 years back and whenever I hear this patriotic song from my favorite Bollywood movie, Naam, I feel both Mother India and my Mother is calling me to come back. A stanza from that song, which is in Hindi, is given below:

Saat Samandar Par Gaya tu
Hum ko zinda mar gaya tu
Desh paraya chod ke aaja
Panchi Pinjra thod ke aaja
Aaja Umar bhaut hai choti
Apne Ghar mein bhi hai Roti

The above stanza means:

You crossed seven seas and went to a foreign land.
Your long absence is killing us.
Leave the foreign country and come back.
Oh Bird, break the cage and come back.
Come back because life is very short
Even in our house we have bread.

I would like my fellow Indians to learn from my life and not be carried away by the glitter of foreign lands, because your true home is where your heart is and in a foreign country, you are always considered as an outsider, at best a second class citizen.

The search for greener pastures on distant shores particularly in the Middle East, can sap the juice of your life and leave you dry because the dream bubble will soon burst. In the Middle East there is no job security and with increased localization of jobs for their own citizens, discrimination, and now with security concerns, Gulf countries should not be on your agenda.

I have seen Indian students all highly qualified and from good families coming to the USA and doing all sorts of odd jobs: waiters, dish washers, gas station attendant etc. Don't get carried away by the exchange rate of a dollar to forty eight Indian rupees. Remember, Sharukh Khan's fate in the famous movie Shakti and with more and more jobs being outsourced to India, it is simply not worth it. Remember, the roads of Dubai, New York and London are not paved with gold, but with struggle and hardship at every step.

I would also like to forward a message to the world leaders that global terrorism can only be reduced when dirty money and questionable financial transactions are targeted, and if the leaders close their eyes and look the other way like Suweidi, events like 9/11 will happen again and again somewhere in the world. Mankind will again suffer and our beautiful world, which started with Eve and Adam, will end with the atom.

Appendix
The Wall Street Journal story
based on my audit report.

U.A.E. Banks Had Suspect Transfers

Central-Bank Documents Show Gulf State Could Be Site for Money Laundering

By Glenn R. Simpson and Erik Portanger

Wednesday, September 17, 2003

To U.S. and global financial-crime investigators, no country in the Middle East is more important than the tiny United Arab Emirates, the financial hub of the Persian Gulf with a long history of lax regulation and a role as a conduit for the Sept. 11, 2001, hijackers.

But as world economic economic leaders gather in the U.A.E. city of Dubai in the next few days, internal documents from the country's central bank show that hundreds of millions of dollars in suspicious funds flowed through accounts at U.A.E. banks during the past few years. The documents highlight how big a challenge the U.A.E. faces in clamping down on money laundering, which it has been attempting to do under pressure from the U.S. and others.

The documents, for instance, provide details of two accounts linked to a British financier who has admitted to hiding money for a jailed U.S. stock promoter. One bank examiner's memo from last year says those accounts, through which more than $90 million flowed between 2000 and 2002, "apparently" were opened at the request of a senior member of the U.A.E.'s ruling family, Sultan bin

Khalifa al Nayhan, and weren't subject to normal inquiries about the account holder.

Another memo details account activity at a local U.A.E. branch of HSBC Holdings PLC, the London-based financial-services company; law- enforcement officials say the branch was tied to international arms dealer Victor Bout. Mr. Bout owns an airline that the United Nations alleges has shipped weapons to Charles Taylor, the former president of Liberia now under indictment for war crimes. Mr. Bout has been indicted in Belgium on money-laundering offenses.

An examiner's memo from 2000 describes a flow of $343 million a year through another HSBC personal account in the U.A.E. The memo states that the turnover was "out of all proportion" to the account holder's stated occupation of "salesman."

Some of the transactions, recently forwarded to U.S. officials, are being examined for possible wrongdoing by investigators at the U.S. Federal Reserve and the U.S. Bureau of Immigration and Customs Enforcement, U.S. officials said.

A spokesman for HSBC declined to comment on the specific accounts, but said the bank wasn't aware of any prosecutions or related investigations that resulted from information it provided to U.A.E. central-bank officials.

Nariman Abdulla Kamber, a senior manager at the U.A.E. central bank, said an inquiry by the institution into the HSBC accounts "did not come out with strong evidence that could give grounds for undue concern." She added, "The U.A.E. considers it extremely important to ensure that monies earned through illegal activities abroad are not run through the financial system in the country for the benefit of these criminals, irrespective of where the crime was committed."

In the wake of the September 2001 terrorist attacks on the U.S., central banks and other financial regulators around the globe have been under pressure to clamp down on the flow of terrorist funding and other illegal money. The U.A.E. has tightened its financial controls and is regulating informal exchange houses that can zap money around the globe.

The central bank has doubled to 12 the number of staff with responsibility for unusual or suspicious transactions at financial institutions. In January 2002, it passed anti-money-laundering legislation that allowed it to freeze assets and impose penalties of as many as seven years of imprisonment, seizure of assets and large fines on people found guilty.

But U.A.E. central-bank documents show that people whom international authorities suspect of wrongdoing have made extensive use of the nation's banking system to transfer money both before and since the September 2001 attacks.

A central-bank examiner this past March raised concerns about suspicious accounts at Abu Dhabi Commercial Bank. One of the principal figures associated with the accounts, according to a memo, was British financier Peter Bond. Mr. Bond has given testimony in federal court in New Jersey under a grant of immunity that he helped hide funds for Robert Brennan, a U.S. stock promoter.

The primary account was in the name of a firm called Pennand Inc., which was registered in Liberia, an offshore haven known for its corporate secrecy. The memo said the account was "operated by" Mr. Bond and Christopher Samuelson, two British financiers whom international investigators say operate Valmet Group, an Isle of Man entity. Mr. Brennan was convicted in 2001 of using Valmet to hide $4 million from creditors. Messrs. Bond and Samuelson couldn't be reached for comment.

The U.A.E.'s Ms. Kamber said the matter "was discussed with the senior management of ADCB and the accounts were closed," but that the action "wasn't due to any evidence of money laundering." ADCB management in the U.A.E. couldn't be reached for comment. The examiner's memo didn't elaborate on why the examiner believed the royal-family member was involved, and Ms. Kamber declined to respond to a question about the connection.

The central bank's biggest concerns centered on a web of accounts at HSBC's branch in Sharjah controlled by a group of nationals from Russia and Central Asia. The primary account in the group was held by a firm called San Air General Trading, which U.N. investigators say is controlled by Mr. Bout. According to a U.N. report in 2000, San Air was used to ship weapons to Liberia's Mr. Taylor.

Mr. Bout also has been implicated in shipping weapons to the Taliban and other outlaw regimes. In public statements, he has denied any wrongdoing. Ms. Kamber said the U.A.E. deported Mr. Bout to Russia. She added "his case was known to the central bank for a long time, but his accounts were left open to watch them for the benefit of the U.N."

(See related letter: "Letters to the Editor: Valmet Group Refutes Accusations in Article" -- WSJ Jan. 13, 2004)